Preventing and responding to violence at work

Preventing and responding to violence at work

Kimberly Ann Rogers and Duncan Chappell

INTERNATIONAL LABOUR OFFICE•GENEVA

Rogers, K.A. ; Chappell, D.
Preventing and responding to violence at work
Geneva, International Labour Office, 2003

Guide, occupational safety, violence, personnel policy. 13.04.2

ISBN 92-2-113374-5

ILO Cataloguing in Publication Data

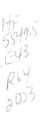

Typeset by Magheross Graphics, France & Ireland *www.magheross.com*
Printod in Great Britain by Biddles Ltd *www.biddles.co.uk*

PREFACE

Workplace violence is one of today's most serious occupational hazards, which can have dire effects on the productivity of organizations, and on the physical and psychological well-being of employees. This book has two simple, yet ambitious, goals: to demonstrate how workplace violence can be prevented by examining how organizations and groups are approaching this serious issue; and to present a reliable and effective methodology for developing workplace violence prevention and response programmes.

It is the responsibility of every employer to provide a safe working environment. For this reason, employers need to take steps to minimize the risk of harm to staff that may result from workplace violence, just as they do with other health and safety hazards. While it is recognized that employers cannot address all the underlying societal factors that contribute to the occurrence of violence at work, there *are* steps that can be taken to reduce the risk of violence in their own working environments.

This book provides direction on how to systematically design and develop workplace violence prevention programmes and policies. This is done by analysing and comparing existing workplace violence prevention guidelines that have been developed across a range of workplaces. Best-practice approaches to responding to workplace violence are reviewed and common themes identified. The book is directed towards all those engaged in combating violence at work, including employers' and workers' organizations, health and safety professionals, consultants, trainers and public policy makers.

This publication stresses the importance of adopting a risk-management approach to workplace violence: one that begins with an appraisal of the nature and scope of the problem, and proceeds to the design, implementation and monitoring of appropriate interventions. Research and experience demonstrate that those organizations which follow the steps in the risk-management process can develop targeted workplace violence prevention programmes that will effectively address the risk factors specific to their working environments. Furthermore, the process presented in this book can and should be adapted for use in any organization (regardless of size, industry or location) where staff are at risk of exposure to violence.

The book is an important part of the ILO's continuing work programme aimed at promoting opportunities for women and men to obtain decent and productive work in conditions of freedom, equity, security and human dignity. In July 1998, the ILO published the first edition of *Violence at work*, a comprehensive report intended to provide a basis for understanding the nature of workplace violence. This study, with its worldwide coverage and focus, demonstrated that violence at work was to be found in both developing and industrialized countries, and in a wide variety of industries and occupations.

Since the publication of *Violence at work*,[1] and perhaps in a small way because of its appearance, there has been a noticeable increase in the international documentation available on this topic, and in the level of resolve displayed by governments, enterprises and workers' representatives to tackle the problems presented by this form of violence. Reflecting these developments, and as an aid to those wishing to explore in greater depth the multidisciplinary literature and issues involved, the ILO's Conditions of Work and Employment Programme has also compiled and published an annotated bibliography on workplace violence.[2] The ILO has developed an interactive educational programme (SOLVE) designed to assist in the development of policy and action to address psychological issues at the workplace, including violence at work. It will also host a Meeting of Experts in October 2003 with the aim of developing a code of practice on violence and stress at work in the service sectors.

To date, the ILO's research in the area of workplace violence has focused primarily on defining and understanding this important issue in an attempt to stimulate action. This book builds on that foundation by taking the next step and focusing on how to prevent and respond to workplace violence. Through the publication of this book, the ILO continues its search for ways to ensure a violence-free workplace and to protect the dignity and equality of all workers. We hope that the book will provide readers with a better understanding of how organizations are approaching this serious issue, and the guidance necessary to initiate the prevention process in their own enterprises.

François Eyraud
Director
Conditions of Work and Employment Programme
International Labour Office

---

[1] Chappell and V. Di Martino: *Violence at work* (Geneva, ILO, 2nd edition, 2000). Also available in French: *La violence au travail* (Geneva, ILO, 2000).

[2] ILO: *Annotated bibliography on violence at work* (Geneva, 1999).

[3] V. Di Martino, D. Gold and A. Schaap: *Managing emerging health-related problems at work*: SOLVE–stress, tobacco, alcohol and drugs, HIV/AIDS, violence (Geneva, ILO, 2002). For further information, see http://www.ilo.org/safework/solve.

CONTENTS

Figures

ABBREVIATIONS

AFL-CIO	American Federation of Labour and Congress of Industrial Organizations
AFSCME	American Federation of State, County and Municipal Employees, AFL-CIO
Cal/OSHA	California Division of Occupational Safety and Health Administration
CCH	Commerce Clearing House International
CCOHS	Canadian Centre for Occupational Health and Safety
EAP	Employee Assistance Program
HSAC	Health and Safety Advisory Committee (United Kingdom)
HSC	Health and Safety Commission (United Kingdom)
HSE	Health and Safety Executive (United Kingdom)
IACP	International Association of Chiefs of Police
IATA	International Air Transport Association
IDS	Incomes Data Services
IRS	Industrial Relations Service
ITF	International Transport Workers Federation
MSF	Manufacturing, Science, Finance Union (United Kingdom)
NCYLC	National Children's and Youth Law Center (New South Wales)
NIOSH	National Institute for Occupational Safety and Health (United States)
NOW	National Organization of Women (United States)
NWNL	Northwestern National Life Insurance Company
OPM	Office of Personnel Management (United States)
OSHA	Occupational Safety and Health Administration (United States)
PERSEREC	Defence Personnel Security Research Centre (United States)
TUC	Trades Union Congress (United Kingdom)
USDAW	Union of Shop, Distributive and Allied Workers (United Kingdom)
WCBBC	Workers' Compensation Board of British Columbia

INTRODUCTION

1

No one expects to be a victim of violence at work. Yet every year, millions of workers around the world experience violent incidents while on the job.[1] Not only is this phenomenon occurring in those workplaces where violence may be expected, such as in prisons, law enforcement and health care, but it has become a danger in many other industries and enterprises. It is a problem of global dimensions that is having a destructive and costly impact upon enterprises in both developing and industrialized nations.[2] It is time for employers to take action to address what is becoming one of today's most pressing workplace issues.

Violence should not be accepted as part of *any job*. Every worker deserves to work in a safe and secure environment where violence is not tolerated, and where respect, equal treatment and productive working relationships are encouraged. *This is attainable*. Research and experience demonstrate that steps can and should be taken to prevent the occurrence of workplace violence within organizations. This book presents these steps and examines how organizations around the world are approaching this serious occupational issue.

About this book

This book provides concrete guidance on how to systematically design, implement and evaluate workplace violence prevention programmes and policies.

---

[1] T. Budd: *Violence at work: Findings from the British Crime Survey* (London, Home Office, 1999); J.A. Kinney and D.L. Johnson: *Breaking point: The workplace violence epidemic and what to do about it* (Chicago, IL, National Safe Workplace Institute, 1993); United States Department of Justice, Bureau of Justice Statistics: *Workplace violence, 1992–96: National crime victimization survey* (Washington, DC, 1998).

[2] B. Ashforth: "Petty tyranny in organizations", in *Human Relations*, Vol. 47, No. 7, 1994, pp. 755–778; J. Barling: "The prediction, experience, and consequences of workplace violence", in E.Q. Bulatao and G.R. VandenBos (eds.): *Violence on the job: Identifying risks and developing solutions* (Washington, DC, American Psychological Association, 1996), pp. 29–49; Kinney and Johnson, op. cit.; Northwestern National Life Insurance Company (NWNL): *Fear and violence in the workplace: A survey documenting the experience of American workers* (Minneapolis, MN, 1993); K.A. Rogers and E.K. Kelloway: "Violence at work: Personal and organizational outcomes", in *Journal of Occupational Health Psychology*, Vol. 12, 1997, pp. 63–71.

This is done by analysing a voluminous and varied set of international resources, policies and guidelines that have been developed across a range of workplaces. The book is directed towards all those engaged in combating violence at work, including employers' and workers' organizations, health and safety professionals, consultants, trainers and public policy makers. It is also directed towards the protection of all workers, including those in "non-standard" forms of employment such as part-time and temporary work – those who, although not defined by law as employees, are in a dependent working relationship – and all those otherwise exposed to risks of violence through their work.

The book is divided into eight chapters:

Chapter 1: *Introduction.* This chapter outlines the purpose and structure of this book, and introduces and defines the issue of workplace violence.

Chapter 2: *Workplace violence prevention – Common themes and guides to policy.* This chapter reviews a number of workplace violence prevention guidelines that have been developed by governments, trade unions, special study groups, workplace violence experts, employers' groups and specific industries. Reference is made to the common themes that emerge from these guidelines, and in particular to the **risk-management approach** to workplace violence prevention. This approach involves a four-step process: (1) assessing and describing the level of risk; (2) designing and implementing appropriate preventive measures; (3) designing and implementing appropriate reactive measures; and (4) monitoring the effectiveness of such preventive and reactive measures. By following this four-step process, organizations can develop workplace violence prevention programmes that effectively identify and address the risk factors specific to their working environments. Each of the steps in the risk-management process is discussed in detail in the four chapters that follow.

Chapter 3: *Step 1 – Assess and describe risk.* The first step in developing workplace violence prevention programmes is that of learning the nature and scope of the problem to be confronted. This chapter provides specific guidance on how to undertake such a risk assessment, including how to choose an assessor, the types of information to collect, the methods and sources for collecting information, and how to analyse the results of the assessment.

Chapter 4: *Step 2 – Design and implement preventive measures.* The goal of any workplace violence prevention programme is to eliminate situations that may result in violence and to reduce the risk of injury or harm. There are many different risk-reduction measures that can help organizations to accomplish this goal, including engineering controls, and work practice or administrative controls. This chapter discusses these different measures and the other two key components of any preventive strategy: a formal system for reporting and investigating incidents of violence; and a process for educating and training those staff who are at risk of violence.

Chapter 5: *Step 3 – Design and implement reactive measures.* Despite the best policies and procedures, incidents of violence can still occur. It is for this reason that a systematic approach to the issue of workplace violence should also include the design and implementation of reactive measures to address incidents as they arise. This chapter discusses how to prepare for, respond to and recover from a critical incident of violence. It further highlights the importance of understanding how such an incident came to pass, so that remedial action can be taken to prevent a similar occurrence in the future.

Chapter 6: *Step 4 – Monitor the effectiveness of preventive and reactive measures.* The fourth and final step in the risk-management process is the evaluation of preventive and reactive measures. This step is extremely important since it is through the evaluation process that an organization determines whether the actions it has taken to eliminate hazards and reduce risk have been successful. This chapter provides guidance on how to evaluate, for example, whether or not preventive measures are actually reducing the frequency and severity of violent incidents. It also suggests ways to assess how effective the reactive measures have been at minimizing the negative outcomes associated with incidents of violence.

Chapter 7: *The risk-management process in review.* This chapter presents case studies of two organizations that have developed workplace violence prevention programmes using a risk-management approach. In so doing, it pulls together the steps in the risk-management process and demonstrates its logical, feasible and flexible nature. This chapter also discusses a number of major and commonly agreed upon principles that should be considered when developing workplace violence prevention programmes, including the importance of eliciting help from groups within the community (e.g. workers' organizations, law enforcement agencies).

Chapter 8: *Conclusion.* This concluding chapter reinforces a number of the key strategies for reducing the risk of workplace violence. Moreover, it reminds readers that workplace violence is indeed preventable and encourages the taking of action to initiate the prevention process.

The changing profile of violence at work

It is a significant challenge to describe and define violence at work. The variety of behaviours that may be included in the definition is great, the boundary between acceptable and unacceptable behaviours is often vague, and per-ceptions in different contexts and cultures of what constitutes violence are diverse. In practice, workplace violence can take many forms, some of which are physical in nature, and some of which are not. Box 1.1 illustrates the wide range of behaviours that are often associated with violence at work.

Public attention has traditionally been focused on physical violence at work.[3] As a result, the common profile that has emerged in the past has been

---

[3] E.Q. Bulatao and G.R. VandenBos: "Workplace violence: Its scope and the issues", in Bulatao and VandenBos, op. cit., pp. 1–23; K.A. Rogers: *Toward an integrative understanding of workplace mistreatment*, unpublished M.A. dissertation (Guelph, Ontario, University of Guelph, 1998).

Box 1.1   Examples of violent behaviours at work

homicide	punching	leaving offensive messages
rape	spitting	aggressive posturing
robbery	scratching	rude gestures
wounding	squeezing, pinching	hostile behaviour
battering	stalking	swearing
physical attacks	bullying	shouting
kicking	mobbing	name-calling
biting	victimizing	innuendo
harassment, including	intimidation	deliberate silence*
sexual and racial abuse	threats	ostracism

*The term "deliberate silence" refers to the practice of socially ostracizing an individual by refusing to speak with him or her for an extended period of time.

Source: adapted from D. Chappell and V. Di Martino: *Violence at work* (Geneva, ILO, 2nd edition, 2000), p. 11.

---

one of extreme violence, often involving deadly force. Although these forms of physical violence have devastating effects on a workplace, and need to be addressed, such incidents are actually quite rare and represent only one of many forms of violence.[4] Evidence has been emerging in more recent years of the harm caused by non-physical forms of violence, referred to under a number of headings including psychological violence,[5] workplace aggression,[6] workplace incivility,[7] emotional abuse,[8] workplace harassment,[9] petty tyranny,[10] counterproductive workplace behaviour[11] and deviant workplace behaviour.[12]

---

[4] Kinney and Johnson, op. cit.

[5] D. Chappell and V. Di Martino: *Violence at work* (Geneva, ILO, 2nd edition, 2000), p. 11.

[6] J.H. Neuman and R.A. Baron: "Aggression in the workplace", in R.A. Giacalone and J. Greenberg: *Antisocial behavior in organizations* (Thousand Oaks, CA, Sage Publications, 1997), pp. 37–67.

[7] L.M. Andersson and C.M. Pearson: "Tit for tat: The spiralling effect of incivility in the workplace", in *Academy of Management Review*, Vol. 24, 1999, pp. 452–471.

[8] L. Keashly: "Emotional abuse in the workplace: Conceptual and empirical issues", in *Journal of Emotional Abuse*, Vol. 1, 1998, pp. 85–117.

[9] L. Keashly and K. Jagatic: "By any other name: American perspectives on workplace bullying", in S. Einarsen et al. (eds.): *Bullying and emotional abuse in the workplace: International perspectives on research and practice* (London, Taylor & Francis, 2003).

[10] Ashforth, op. cit.

[11] S. Fox, P.E. Spector and D. Miles: "Counterproductive work behavior (CWB) in response to job stressors and organizational justice: Some mediator and moderator tests for autonomy and emotions", in *Journal of Vocational Behavior*, Vol. 59, 2001, pp. 291–309.

[12] S.L. Robinson and R.J. Bennett: "A typology of deviant workplace behaviours: A multidimensional scaling study", in *Academy of Management Journal*, Vol. 38, No. 2, 1995, pp. 555–572.

There are a number of reasons why it is important to consider incidents of emotional or psychological violence when discussing workplace violence. First and foremost, there is evidence to suggest that exposure to these incidents, especially over an extended period of time, has detrimental effects on the health and well-being of the victim.[13] Second, psychological violence in the workplace is simply more frequent than physical violence.[14] Third, based on the research on family violence, it is apparent that incidents of psychological violence can and do often precede physical violence.[15] For these reasons, organizations need to work to prevent both physical and non-physical forms of workplace violence.

In an attempt to organize and understand the wide range of behaviours that fall under the heading of workplace violence, a number of typologies have been developed.[16] One of the most useful typologies stems from Baron and Neuman's[17] application of Buss's conceptualization of human aggression to aggressive workplace behaviours. Buss argued that aggressive behaviour could be conceptualized along three dimensions: physical–verbal, active–passive, and direct–indirect. Box 1.2 shows how different violent behaviours at work can be categorized using this typology. Subsequent studies have shown that most violence or aggression occurring in work settings is verbal, indirect and passive in nature, rather than physical, direct and active.[18]

Baron and Neuman make the distinction between workplace violence and workplace aggression. They use workplace aggression as a general term to encompass all forms of behaviour by which individuals attempt to harm others at work or their organizations, and workplace violence as those instances involving direct physical assaults (i.e. they see violence as an example of aggression). For the purposes of this book we will use the term "workplace violence" as our overarching term to describe all the harmful behaviours and events we discuss. We do this for two reasons. First, the term violence carries with it a more powerful connotation than does aggression – it communicates that a range of aggressive behaviours can hurt and cause major damage to people. Second, making the distinction between physical and non-physical examples of violence makes little sense given that most acts of physical violence almost always involve verbal or emotional violence. To create and highlight a distinction between non-physical events (aggression) and physical

---

[13] Ashforth, op. cit.; L. Keashly and K. Jagatic: *The nature, extent, and impact of emotional abuse in the workplace: Results of a statewide survey*, unpublished paper, presented at an Academy of Management conference, Toronto, 2000; H. Leymann: "Mobbing and psychological terror at workplaces", in *Violence and Victims*, Vol. 5, No. 2, 1990, pp. 119–126; C. Rayner, H. Hoel and C.L. Cooper: *Workplace bullying: What we know, who is to blame, and what can we do?* (London, Taylor & Francis, 2002).

[14] R.A. Baron and J.H. Neuman: "Workplace violence and workplace aggression: Evidence on their relative frequency and potential causes", in *Aggressive Behavior*, Vol. 22, 1996, pp. 161–173; Rogers, op. cit.

[15] Barling, op. cit.

[16] ibid.; Bulatao and VandenBos, op. cit.; Kinney and Johnson, op. cit.

[17] Baron and Neuman, op. cit.; A.H. Buss: *The psychology of aggression* (New York, Wiley, 1961).

[18] Baron and Neuman, op. cit.; Rogers, op. cit.

Box 1.2 Examples of eight types of workplace aggression	
Type of aggression	*Examples*
Verbal–passive–indirect	Failing to deny false rumours about the target Failing to transmit information needed by the target
Verbal–passive–direct	Failing to return phone calls Giving someone "the silent treatment"
Verbal–active–indirect	Spreading false rumours about the target Belittling someone's opinions to others
Verbal–active–direct	Insults; yelling, shouting Flaunting status or authority; acting in a condescending way
Physical–passive–indirect	Causing others to delay action on matters of importance to the target Failing to take steps that would protect the target's welfare or safety
Physical–passive–direct	Purposely leaving a work area when target enters Reducing others' opportunities to express themselves
Physical–active–indirect	Theft or destruction of property belonging to the target Needlessly consuming resources needed by the target
Physical–active–direct	Physical attack (e.g. pushing, shoving, hitting) Negative or obscene gestures toward the target

Source: adapted from Baron and Neuman, 1996, op. cit., p. 164.

events (violence) does not recognize the intimate connections between these different forms of violence.

Another important distinction made in the research literature, and key to understanding the dynamics involved in workplace violence, is between that violence which comes from employees internal to the organization, and that which comes from outside the organization (e.g. clients, customers, thieves, terrorists). The former may be referred to as "organization-motivated" violence and the latter as "occupational" violence.[19] Given that the motives associated with organization-motivated events differ from those associated

---

[19] J.H. Neuman and R.A. Baron: "Workplace violence and workplace aggression: Evidence concerning specific forms, potential causes, and preferred targets", in *Journal of Management*, Vol. 24, No. 3, 1998, pp. 391–419.

with occupational violence, this distinction has important implications for the prevention and management of these serious acts. Researchers from the California Department of Industrial Relations in the United States have recognized this important distinction, and have suggested three broad categories of work-related violence, based on the source of the violence, which can help understand this issue, and develop strategies to prevent violence at work:[20]

Type 1 – Criminal intruder: incidents involving agents or perpetrators who had no legitimate nexus to the organization or workplace, e.g. bank robbers

Type 2 – Client or customer: incidents where the perpetrator was the recipient of some service provided by the organization, e.g. current or former clients, patients and customers

Type 3 – Internal employee: incidents where the perpetrator was in some form of employment or past-employment relationship with the affected workplace, e.g. co-workers or supervisors

Not only do the motives differ depending on the source of violence (e.g. a robber is after money, while a customer might be trying to secure a service), but so do the forms of violence used and the associated risks. Research shows that physical forms of violence, for example, come most frequently from outside the organization (either Type 1 or 2) and not from disgruntled employees.[21] Moreover, verbal and emotional forms of violence (threats, intimidation, name-calling) tend to be more salient when they come from co-workers (Type 3), rather than from members of the public.[22]

Particular attention has been focused upon psychological violence that is perpetrated through repeated behaviour of a type which, by itself, may be relatively minor, but which cumulatively can become very serious, such as workplace bullying or mobbing. Bullying is usually defined as a subset of aggressive behaviour, in which the aggression is repeated and occurs over an extended period of time, and in which there is an imbalance of power such that it is difficult for the victim to defend him/herself.[23] By its nature, bullying is predicated on an ongoing series of negative interactions that occurs within a specific relationship. The key to understanding bullying, unlike some other forms of workplace violence, then becomes the frequency and duration of the act, rather than the severity of the individual behaviours. Since bullying is substantially different from isolated violent behaviours, policies and programmes aimed at this particular form of workplace violence should be based on an understanding of its unique characteristics.

---

[20] California Department of Industrial Relations, Division of Occupational Safety and Health Administration (Cal/OSHA): *Guidelines for workplace security* (San Francisco, CA, 1995) (hereafter Cal/OSHA guide). This document is available from the following website: http://165.235.90.100/DOSH/dosh_publications/worksecurity.html.

[21] Bulatao and VandenBos, op. cit.; NWNL, op. cit.; Rogers, op. cit.

[22] Rogers, op. cit.

[23] H. Cowie et al.: "Measuring workplace bullying", in *Aggression and Violent Behavior*, Vol. 7, 2002, pp. 33–51.

An integrated definition of workplace violence

The contemporary profile of violence at work gives due recognition to physical and psychological behaviours, but also incorporates minor acts of violence.[24] While this profile is now more fully and appropriately delineated, consensus has yet to emerge regarding a general definition of workplace violence. To date, no such definition has been agreed upon in the international arena, although the European Commission, which has proposed the following definition, has made substantial progress: "Incidents where persons are abused, threatened or assaulted in circumstances relating to their work, involving an explicit or implicit challenge to their safety, well-being and health".[25]

This definition covers a wide spectrum of violent incidents and illustrates the trend at the international level towards a broad, inclusive definition of workplace violence. This trend is further reflected in many of the preventive guidelines discussed throughout this book. Following this integrated definition, the book outlines strategies to prevent and respond to a wide range of violent incidents at work (Types 1, 2 and 3 as well as physical and verbal forms). While it is critical to try to prevent intruders and customers from being violent or abusive, it is equally important to address worker-on-worker violence, where organizations may be able to exert a more direct and lasting influence on prevention.

The causes of violence

Just as many practitioners and researchers in this area have taken a broad approach to the *definition* of violence, they have also recognized the importance of taking a comprehensive approach to understanding the causes of violence at work. The causes of these behaviours are complex and defy easy explanation. Much time and energy have been spent trying to identify those individual factors associated with the assailant, in an attempt to arrive at a "typical" profile.[26] The limited value of this approach has been recognized, and today it is widely accepted by the scientific community engaged in violence-related research that a number of important factors and circumstances contribute to any particular incident of workplace violence. Among these contributing factors are attributes associated with the assailant and the victim, as well as aspects of the working environment and the surrounding community.[27]

These factors must all be kept in mind when trying to understand workplace violence, and even more importantly, when trying to prevent and respond to it. This means that instead of searching for a single solution to any particular violent situation, the full range of causes should be analysed and a range of interventions, control and prevention measures applied. These measures should

---

[24] Chappell and Di Martino, op. cit., p. 14.

[25] R. Wynne et al.: *Guidance on the prevention of violence at work* (Brussels, European Commission, 1997), p. 1.

[26] Kinney and Johnson, op. cit.

[27] See Chappell and Di Martino, op. cit.

seek to instil a broad preventive approach to the problem – one that addresses the individual, interpersonal, organizational and cultural roots of the violence.[28] The utility of examining all the underlying causes and the full range of preventive measures is an important theme that runs throughout this book. Please note that a more detailed discussion of the explanations behind the phenomenon of workplace violence is presented in Appendix B for those readers who would like to explore this area further.

While dialogue may continue in a number of forums about the precise way in which workplace violence should be defined and the specific factors which contribute to its occurrence, there would seem to be a consensus that this form of violence is:

- a major, although still under-recognized, problem;
- not limited to individual catastrophes, such as mass homicide, but extends to a much wider range of apparently minor but often devastating behaviours;
- an extremely costly burden for the worker, the enterprise and the community;
- not just an episodic, individual problem, but a structural, strategic problem rooted in wider social, economic, organizational and cultural factors; and
- detrimental to the functioning of the affected workplace, such that any action taken against such violence is an integral part of the organizational development of a sound enterprise.[29]

Towards prevention

A key precursor to the development of any effective workplace violence prevention programme is a basic understanding of the actions that comprise workplace violence, and the factors that contribute to its occurrence. The aim of this introductory chapter has been to provide this basic level of understanding and to set the parameters for the detailed review that follows. This review will examine the responses made by a broad spectrum of occupational groups, organizations and jurisdictions to combat workplace violence. As will become evident, these responses typically involve the development of guidelines, policies and related aids to action.

The development and implementation of corporate policies and guidelines represent just one of a number of approaches that can be adopted to manage this serious problem. Another approach is the introduction of legislative measures. In some European countries, for example, specific regulatory responsibilities have been assigned in regard to workplace violence.[30] In most European jurisdictions, however, this area is covered only in non-specific terms by health and safety laws, or in various civil and criminal statutes. A similar situation

[28] ibid., p. 15.
[29] ibid.
[30] ibid., Ch. 4.

prevails elsewhere at the national level, although recent research suggests that in both Europe and other regions of the world, more localized and focused initiatives are now being implemented. These initiatives have tended to be sector specific, and are usually supported by a state agency in participation with trade unions and other worker-based groups.[31]

In the longer term, as knowledge of the nature of workplace violence grows and greater consensus is reached about the operational definition of the phenomenon, it seems likely that national, regional and international bodies will become more directly involved in the articulation of specific prevention strategies. Meanwhile, much that is relevant and of practical benefit can be learned from the more localized guidelines on "best practice" approaches that have already been produced. These guidelines are reviewed in the next chapter.

---

[31] H. Standing and D. Nicolini: *Review of workplace-related violence* (London, Health and Safety Executive (HSE), 1997), p. 47.

WORKPLACE VIOLENCE PREVENTION: COMMON THEMES AND GUIDES TO POLICY

2

Starting the process

What is the appropriate point at which to begin the process of developing plans to prevent and respond to workplace violence? The simple answer to this question is that an organization or enterprise should seek to commence this process well before a risk of violence becomes a reality. All too frequently an organization or enterprise will address this issue only after experiencing a violent incident, and in an atmosphere that is still charged with the emotion provoked by that incident. In such an atmosphere the temptation may well be to resort to immediate and simple solutions to deal with the perceived problem.

A basic message or theme for anyone involved in any planning in this field is that there are no easy solutions or short cuts, just as there are no universal blueprints for dealing with the risk of violence at work.[1] In reality, what works for one organization often does not work for another. There are a number of important factors that influence how an organization should act to address this important issue, and that explain why an intervention might work in one company and not in another. Among these factors are:

- the level and nature of risk that exists within the organization;
- the nature of the operation;
- the organizational culture, including employee dynamics;
- the size of the organization;
- the location of the organization and the workforce (centralized or decentralized?);
- its hours of operation; and

---

[1] UNISON: *Violence at work: A guide to risk prevention for UNISON branches, stewards and safety representatives* (London, 1997), p. 15 (hereafter UNISON guide).

- the legal requirements related to workplace violence in the country or jurisdiction.[2]

Most commentators agree that central to the management of work-related violence is the need for a planned and systematic approach to the assessment of the problem and the implementation of effective prevention strategies.[3] Indeed, the International Labour Organization's SOLVE programme advocates an integrated approach towards addressing a range of psychosocial issues – violence, stress, alcohol and drugs, HIV/AIDS and tobacco – and takes into account the interrelationships between them and the cause and effect patterns relevant to each.[4] Moreover, single and simple solutions, such as the installation of panic buttons that can be activated in a crisis situation, are neither appropriate nor responsible ways of responding to the complex issue of violence at work. Rather, written policies and procedures need to be developed which allow organizations and their staff to appreciate and understand the boundaries of their respective roles and responsibilities.

It is also commonly agreed that the involvement of workers is crucial in establishing an effective violence prevention programme.[5] Without their input and support it is nearly impossible to identify the actual risks facing the organization and to successfully implement preventive measures. It should therefore be ensured that workers are consulted, informed and trained on this issue and that their representatives have the time and resources to participate actively in the processes of organizing, planning, implementing, evaluating and improving the violence prevention programme.[6] In unionized environments, it is important to involve the union early on in the process of planning so that it can have an opportunity to express workers' concerns and to bring to bear its expertise and knowledge.[7]

Learning from existing guidelines and policies

Over the past decade, and at a rapidly accelerating pace in more recent years, a rich and varied range of guidelines and policies has been developed that seek

---

[2] S. Perrone: *Violence in the workplace*, Research and Public Policy Series, No. 22 (Canberra, Australian Institute of Criminology, 1999), p. 74; Canadian Centre for Occupational Health and Safety (CCOHS): *Violence in the workplace: Prevention guide* (Hamilton, Ontario, 2nd edition, 2001), "How do I use this guide?" (hereafter CCOHS guide).

[3] H. Standing and D. Nicolini: *Review of workplace-related violence* (London, HSE, 1997), p. 47.

[4] V. Di Martino, D. Gold and A. Schaap: *Managing emerging health-related problems at work* (Geneva, ILO, 2002). For further information see http://www.ilo.org/safework/solve

[5] United States Department of Labor, Occupational Safety and Health Administration (OSHA): *Guidelines for preventing workplace violence for health care and social service workers* (Washington, DC, 1998), pp. 2–3 (hereafter OSHA health care guidelines).

[6] International Labour Office (ILO): *Guidelines on occupational safety and health management systems, ILO–OSH 2001* (Geneva, 2001) (hereafter ILO–OSH 2001); see http//www.ilo.org/public/english/protection/safework/managmnt/guide.htm

[7] UNISON, op. cit., p. 16.

to deal with issues associated with work-related violence. These pre-existing guidelines and policies can serve as an invaluable and comprehensive source of assistance to organizations developing workplace violence prevention strategies. It should be stressed that nomenclature in this area is frequently imprecise, and the terms "guideline" and "policy" are often used interchangeably. In this book, however, when the term "guideline" is used it is intended to describe a document which conveys quite general information and advice about how best to respond to violence at work, including how to develop appropriate policies and procedures. "Policy", on the other hand, is a term that usually describes and reflects the outcome of any guidance received, with more focused and specific information, advice and procedures being directed at a designated audience.

In the earlier ILO study, *Violence at work*, a selected list of published guidelines was presented.[8] This list remains indicative rather than definitive of the vast array of published documents and information which is now available, in both printed and electronic forms, about ways of responding to different aspects of workplace violence. They can and do offer helpful and comprehensive advice and assistance to any organization or individual seeking to develop more specific policies and procedures to manage work-related violence. The information and examples in those guidelines will be used throughout this book to illustrate the range of approaches and measures that can be exercised in the prevention of workplace violence.

It is important to make a cautionary note at this point. While these existing guidelines can provide "operational benchmarks" and interesting examples from which to work, their role is not to supply off-the-shelf template solutions. As with the use of best practices in other areas, such as marketing, the focus should be on understanding process rather than copying detail. When developing a workplace violence prevention programme it is imperative that organizations make discernible judgements based on the peculiarities of their particular working environments.[9]

A number of the guidelines contained in the selected list of published guidelines have already had a far-reaching influence and impact upon the overall development of prevention strategies in this area. For example, the work of the United States Department of Labor's Occupational Safety and Health Administration (OSHA), and the National Institute for Occupational Safety and Health (NIOSH), has for a number of years provided a benchmark framework for preventing violence in certain high-risk occupations and situations. In Europe, the contributions made by the British Health and Safety Executive (HSE), and by the Tavistock Institute, have already been acknowledged. Major union groups in the United Kingdom, such as the Trades Union Congress (TUC), the Manufacturing, Science, Finance Union (MSF) and UNISON (representing public service workers) have also produced valuable guidelines

---

[8] D. Chappell and V. Di Martino: *Violence at work* (Geneva, 2nd edition, 2000), pp. 108–110.

[9] Perrone, op. cit., p. 75.

dealing with particular issues, including bullying and various forms of work-place harassment.

It will be noticed that the sources of the guidelines are, without exception, located in the industrialized countries of the world. There is at present a serious deficiency in the information available about the nature and scope of workplace violence in less-developed countries, as reflected in the current absence of published guidelines originating from such countries. This deficiency is a matter of concern, not least because there is every reason to believe that problems of workplace violence are as real and immediate in developing countries as they are in the developed parts of the world, while the specific responses required to deal with these problems may be dissimilar. Thus the utility and relevance of the listed guidelines to less-developed countries are at present a matter of conjecture.

This being said, it is likely that the basic preventive, or risk-management, approach presented below and discussed throughout this book will work well in both developing and industrialized settings. It is modelled on the risk-management approach adopted and successfully implemented around the world to address other health and safety hazards. Even if the nature of the violence that occurs within organizations differs across countries (possibly due to societal or ethnic differences), and even if the specific preventive measures necessary to control the issue differ, the steps in developing an effective prevention programme are likely to be the same.

A risk-management framework

While divergent approaches and policies continue to exist in the responses made to the prevention of work-related violence, one common theme which does emerge from the more influential guidelines is the utility of adopting an occupational health and safety risk-management framework in this area.[10] A risk-management framework identifies a recursive cycle of activities to ensure continuous improvement in the assessment and management of risk, beginning with an appraisal of the nature and scope of the problem, and followed by the design, implementation and evaluation of appropriate preventive measures. It is commonly agreed among researchers and practitioners in this area that by following a risk-management process an organization can develop a targeted workplace violence prevention programme that will effectively address the risk factors specific to their working environment.[11] In so doing, organizations meet the need for a systematic approach to the handling of violence at work. It is

---

[10] Standing and Nicolini, op. cit., pp. 47–48; Chappell and Di Martino, op. cit., Ch. 5; R.Wynne et al.: *Guidance on the prevention of violence at work* (Brussels, European Commission, 1996), pp. 18–19.

[11] B. Poyner and C. Warne: *Preventing violence to staff* (London, HSE, 1988); American Federation of State, County and Municipal Employees (AFSCME), AFL-CIO: *Preventing workplace violence* (Washington, DC, 1998) (hereafter AFSCME guide) (available from http://www.afscme.org/health/violtc.htm); WorkSafe Western Australia Commission: *Workplace violence: Code of practice* (Perth, Government of Western Australia, 1999) (hereafter Western Australian code of practice); see http://www.safetyline.wa.gov.au/pagebin/pg000047.htm.

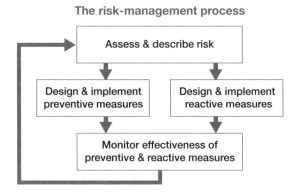

The risk-management process

important to recognize that the risk-management process is a method for identifying and controlling the risk of workplace violence, and as such it provides guidance on how to develop a prevention programme, but not on *what* should be included in the programme. The risk-management framework or process has been favourably considered by influential bodies,[12] and is adapted for use in the presentation of subsequent sections of this book.

Proponents of the risk-management framework differ slightly in their identification and description of the particular types of activities and phases contained in the process.[13] The process outlined above contains the key components from most of the risk-management frameworks and resembles most closely (in condensed form) the steps suggested by Chappell and Di Martino[14] and the European Commission.[15]

Assess and describe risk: The purpose of this step is to collect data in order to assess the risk of violence within the workplace, and to understand the nature of the hazards responsible for this risk. Activities may include:[16]

- determining the level of risk of violence within the working environment;
- describing the existing hazards and the nature of risk.

Design and implement preventive measures: The purpose of this step is to develop and implement a targeted programme (based on the results of the risk assessment) to prevent or minimize the risk of workplace violence. Activities may include:[17]

- searching for possible measures to prevent violence (e.g. changes to the physical environment, changes to the way work is organized, changes to policies, etc.);

---

[12] Wynne et al., op. cit. See also ILO–OSH 2001, op. cit.

[13] See, for example, the contrasting views in D. Beale, T. Cox and P. Leather: "Work-related violence: Is national reporting good enough?", in *Work and Stress*, Vol. 10, No. 2, 1996, pp. 99–103; and Wynne et al., op. cit.

[14] Chappell and Di Martino, op. cit., p. 106.

[15] Wynne et al., op. cit., p. 43.

[16] Chappell and Di Martino, op. cit., p. 106.

[17] Wynne et al., op. cit., p. 43.

- working collaboratively to choose the most effective measures;
- implementing measures in a visible way.

Design and implement reactive measures: Although an organization's primary goal should always be to prevent violence at work, it is also important to have reactive measures in place in the unfortunate case of an incident. This part of the process focuses on the design and implementation of these reactive measures. Activities may include:[18]

- searching for potential reactive and protective interventions (e.g. critical incident preparation, post-trauma support, complaint investigation);
- deciding on interventions in a collaborative way;
- implementing measures.

Monitor effectiveness of preventive and reactive measures: The purpose of this final step is to assess the effectiveness of the preventive measures in reducing the number of violent incidents that occur, and to assess the ability of the reactive measures to minimize the negative outcomes associated with actual events. Activities may include:

- monitoring the measures in terms of process and outcome;
- identifying/modifying those interventions in need of improvement or replacement;
- publicizing the results of the monitoring.

There are two other important features of the risk-management process that are worthy of discussion at this point. The first is the cyclical nature of the process. The risk-management process is one that should be revisited periodically. Once preventive measures are implemented and evaluated, risks must once again be assessed. Any new or ongoing risks identified in this process must then be addressed. The second noteworthy feature of this process is its flexibility. Although there is agreement that at a basic level risk must be assessed and preventive measures implemented and evaluated, there is a lot of flexibility in the way these steps are accomplished (e.g. the process may be simpler for smaller companies). This flexibility will become even more apparent in the subsequent chapters that describe differing approaches to the various steps in the process. It is very important that organizations adapt the risk-management process, and the resulting preventive measures, to their own needs.

Of the guidelines identified and discussed earlier, most endorse and apply directly a risk-management framework, whether addressing themselves to special risk situations, special types of violence or more general audiences. In the general category, six guidelines have been singled out for specific and detailed mention in this book because of their particular and insightful consideration of the issues associated with workplace violence. These guidelines are the

---

[18] ibid.

Western Australian code of practice;[19] the United States Office of Personnel Management (OPM) guide;[20] the American Federation of State, County and Municipal Employees (AFSCME) guide;[21] the University of California at Berkeley's Labor and Occupational Health Program guide;[22] the OSHA workplace violence prevention programme elements;[23] and the Canadian Centre for Cccupational Health and Safety (CCOHS) guide.[24]

Each of the six guides mentioned offers practical and broadly based advice about how to go about formulating detailed policies and procedures to prevent workplace violence. It is now proposed to review that advice, in tandem with material drawn from other guidelines, under the four broad headings corresponding to the steps in the risk-management framework, as outlined earlier in this chapter:

- Assess and describe risk
- Design and implement preventive measures
- Design and implement reactive measures
- Monitor effectiveness of preventive and reactive measures.

---

[19] Western Australian code of practice, op. cit., p. 1. This code is intended to suggest principles for application to a very wide range of workplaces and jurisdictions where violent incidents may arise. It has the status of a formal code of practice under the provisions of Western Australia's Occupational Safety and Health Act 1984 and Occupational Safety and Health Regulations 1996.

[20] United States Office of Personnel Management, Office of Workplace Relations: *Dealing with workplace violence: A guide for agency planners*, doc. No. OWR-09 (Washington, DC, 1998) (hereafter OPM guide); see http://www.opm.gov/workplac/pdf/full.pdf. This guide is an authoritative and very comprehensive reference aid prepared to help United States' federal agency planners deal with workplace violence. The guidance is based on the collective expertise and experience of federal government law enforcement officers, security specialists, criminal investigators, attorneys, employee relations specialists, employee assistance programme counsellors, forensic psychologists and union officials. It consists primarily of "lessons learned" from many years of experience with actual cases involving potentially violent and violent employees. The guidance covers incidents of physical violence, as well as of intimidation and "bullying".

[21] AFSCME guide, op. cit. This guide is the product of a large AFL-CIO affiliated public workers' union in the United States with specific concerns about the threat posed by workplace violence to the security and welfare of its members. It contains a number of practical suggestions about prevention strategies for dealing with particular types of violence, as well as pointing to various pitfalls to be avoided in the violence prevention planning process.

[22] University of California at Berkeley, Labor Occupational Health Program: *Violence on the job: A guidebook for labor and management* (Berkeley, CA, Center for Occupational and Environmental Health, 1997) (hereafter Berkeley guide). This guide was prepared with the assistance of a task force of union members in California, and reviewed by an impressive array of persons in labour, management, government and other positions in the United States (see http://socrates.berkeley.edu/~lohp/Publications/Violence-on-the-Job/violence- on-the-job.htm).

[23] These basic, common elements of an effective workplace violence prevention programme are derived from United States Department of Labor, Occupational Safety and Health Administration (OSHA): *Workplace violence awareness and prevention* (Washington, DC, 1998), pp. 1–2 (hereafter OSHA workplace violence guide); see http://www.osha-slc.gov/workplace_violence/wrkplaceViolence.Table.html. This guide represents one, albeit the most comprehensive, of a number of highly regarded research-based documents dealing with workplace violence prepared by this federal occupational health and safety agency for widespread distribution and use in the United States. Despite its North American orientation the guide contains a wealth of general advice and information that can be utilized in many settings far removed from its originating source.

[24] CCOHS guide, op. cit. A product of Canada's national Centre for Occupational Health and Safety, this guide is unique in being published in a readily carried pocket size. It states that the information it contains has been organized to support the development of workplace-specific violence prevention programmes across business sectors and occupational groupings.

STEP 1 – ASSESS AND DESCRIBE RISK

3

The risk-management process

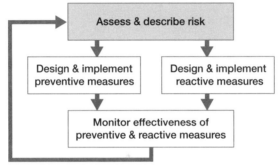

Purpose of the risk-assessment phase

The first step in developing any policies and procedures to prevent and respond to violence in the workplace is that of finding out the nature and scope of the problem to be confronted. Without this information it is impossible to develop a targeted prevention strategy that will successfully address the hazards specific to an organization.

Two basic questions need to be answered through this first step in the risk-management process:

1. *What is the level and nature of risk within the working environment?* It is extremely important to understand the hazards that exist within the working environment and the risks of injury or harm associated with exposure to these hazards. The level of risk can range from relatively small to very large.

2. *Are there any policies, procedures or systems already in existence within the organization that help to eliminate or minimize the risk of violence?* For example, it would be important to assess the success of any pre-existing

security systems at minimizing the risk of violence from the external environment, or the success of internal policies at minimizing the risk of worker-on-worker violence.

In a small enterprise, this first step in the risk-management process may not be very complex or time-consuming. In larger organizations, however, an assessment of the risks involved may require a significant commitment of both time and resources. It is clear that no two workplaces will face exactly the same hazards or level of risk, but extensive general guidance is available to assist organizations and individuals wishing to undertake a risk assessment. Much of this guidance is shared in this chapter under the following headings:

• Choosing an assessor
• Establishing an approach or framework
   – Types of information to collect
   – Methods and sources
   – Organizing and summarizing results
   – Examples of risk-assessment tools

Important Distinction: Hazard versus Risk

Hazard: Anything that can cause harm
Risk: The chance that someone will be harmed by the hazard
and the potential severity of harm

Choosing an assessor

It is very important to select carefully the person(s) who will perform the risk assessment since this step serves as the foundation for the violence prevention programme. There are a couple of things to consider when making this decision.[1] First, a risk assessment can be conducted by either an individual or a team. The larger the organization the greater the need for a team approach. If a team approach is chosen, the organization may wish to draw the team members from different parts of the enterprise (e.g. Operations, Security, Human Resources, the union, etc.).

Second, the individual(s) chosen should have strong analytical and systems thinking, be thorough and detail oriented, be respected and trusted within the organization, and have the ability to persuade others to accept their

---

[1] United States Department of Labor, Occupational Safety and Health Administration (OSHA): *Recommendations for workplace violence prevention programmes in late-night retail establishments* (Washington, DC, 1998), p. 4 (hereafter OSHA late-night retail guide) (see http://www.osha-slc.gov/SLTC/workplaceviolence/latenight); B. Poyner and C. Warne: *Preventing violence to staff* (London, HSE, 1988), pp. 8–12; J. Gallagher: *Violent times. A health and safety report* (London, TUC, 1999), p. 24.

recommendations. This latter requirement is particularly important since consultation with staff and managers throughout the risk-assessment process is critical, both for creating the best possible picture of the likely risks, and for gaining cooperation from staff in implementing the strategy that results. Some guidelines go further to suggest that the individual(s) responsible for the risk assessment should also be responsible for the design and implementation of the prevention strategy.

Establishing an approach or a framework

Before starting a risk assessment, the assessor needs a clear idea of his/her key questions and desired outcomes (box 3.1). This way the risk assessment will be targeted and relevant to the particular situation. For example, most risk assessments seek to identify the occupations/groups and locations within the enterprise that are most at risk of violence. The CCOHS guide describes specific

---

Box 3.1   Framework for a workplace violence risk assessment

Look for trends. Identify occupations and locations which are most at risk:

- How many incidents of violence in the workplace have been documented or reported in your workplace or in related workplaces?
- How many incidents of potentially violent situations, such as threats, have been documented or reported in your workplace or in related workplaces?
- What occupational groups or individual employees appear to be most at risk, in terms of either frequency or severity of violence or potential violence?
- How many of the incidents involved:
  - verbal abuse or threats?
  - physically threatening behaviour?
  - harassment?
- Is there any particular location that appears to have experienced a higher proportion of incidents of violence?
- Is there a time of day, month or year when incidents of violence have occurred more often?

Categorize the degree of risk for different areas or occupations:

- **high risk** – one or more contributing factors frequently place the employee at serious risk and/or the risk is severe.
- **moderate risk** – the employee is at risk on a less frequent basis and/or the risk is less than severe.
- **low risk** – employees are rarely or never exposed to risk and/or the risk in minimal.

Source: adapted from CCOHS guide, 1999, op. cit., pp. 14–15.

---

questions that should be answered as a part of any risk assessment, and suggests that an attempt be made to categorize the degree of risk for different areas or occupations within the workplace.

There is a variety of ways to organize risk assessment information in order to understand the nature of risk within a working environment (e.g. by groups at risk, by hazard). It is helpful to identify an approach or framework for organizing this information in advance, so as to guarantee that the assessor collects all the relevant information. One potentially useful means for organizing and analysing risk-assessment results is by examining the three broad categories (sources) of work-related violence proposed by the researchers from the California Department of Industrial Relations in the United States (these are presented below). This categorization can be helpful in describing and understanding the extent and nature of violence within an enterprise, and in developing strategies to prevent violence at work:[2]

Type 1 – Criminal intruder: incidents involving agents or perpetrators who have no legitimate nexus to the organization or workplace, e.g. robbers

Type 2 – Client or customer: incidents where the perpetrator is the recipient of some service provided by the organization, e.g. current or former clients, patients, customers

Type 3 – Internal employee: incidents where the perpetrator is in some form of present or post-employment relationship with the affected workplace, i.e. co-workers or supervisors

This categorization provides a useful framework through which to understand who is at risk of what within the working environment. Figure 3.1 provides an example of a template that could be used to document those work groups within the organization who are at risk of workplace violence, the types of violence each is at risk of, and the level of risk. By identifying the types of violent incidents that have occurred in the past, and those types of incidents that

Figure 3.1   Risk-assessment template – an example

Groups at risk within company	Types of violence			Level of risk (high, medium, low)
	Type 1: External perpetrator	Type 2: Client or customer	Type 3: Internal employees	
Staff in Finance Department			✔	Medium
Staff in remote locations	✔	✔		Medium
Front-line staff	✔	✔		High

---

[2] Cal/OSHA guide, op. cit.

workers are at risk of experiencing in the future, assessors can start planning appropriate preventive action.

Another approach or framework for recording risk-assessment information is provided by the Western Australian code of practice. Its Hazard Identification Worksheet (a completed example relating to a small retail enterprise is provided in figure 3.2, and a blank example is provided in figure 3.4) provides a framework through which specific hazards can be identified, as well as the number of people affected and the frequency of each hazard.

Although this example focuses on incidents of Type 1 (robbers) and Type 2 (customers) violence, it would be easy to expand this worksheet to include incidents of Type 3 (employee) violence and associated hazards.

Once an assessor has identified specific questions and an approach/framework, he or she is ready to start collecting information and data. Having a clear idea of what is wanted at the end of the assessment allows the assessor(s) to identify which information to collect in order to address these questions and complete any relevant templates. The next section describes the range of information that can be collected.

Types of information to collect

Various types of information can be collected when assessing an organization's level of risk. That being said, most of the information that is discussed and suggested within the guidelines on preventing workplace violence can be grouped under one of the following categories:

- *Past incidents of violence:*[4] It is commonly agreed that one of the most important pieces of information to collect during the risk-assessment phase is information on past incidents of workplace violence (both actual incidents and near misses). This information will give the assessor(s) an idea of recurring problems and trends, as well as of how well the organization responds to incidents of violence. Information on the frequency, severity and location of past incidents will be helpful, as will information on who is being victimized and by whom.

- *Environmental and organizational features that put employees at risk:*[5] Key to any risk assessment of this nature is an understanding of the factors in an organization's external and internal environments that put employees at risk of workplace violence (e.g. layout of the workplace and surrounding area, nature of work processes and client groups). Many of these "risk factors" are

---

[4] A. Ishmael with B. Alemoru: *Harassment, bullying and violence at work: A practical guide to combating employee abuse* (London, The Industrial Society, 1999), pp. 151–154; S. Perrone: *Violence at the workplace*, Research and Public Policy Series, No. 22 (Canberra, Australian Institute of Criminology, 1999), pp. 78–80; CCOHS guide, op. cit., pp. 10–14; Workers' Compensation Board of British Columbia (WCBBC): *Take care: How to develop and implement a workplace violence program* (Vancouver, 2001), p. 11 (hereafter WCBBC guide); http://worksafebc.com/publications/publication-index/t.asp.

[5] Perrone, op. cit., pp. 78–80; WCBBC guide, op. cit., p. 11; UNISON guide, op. cit., p. 18; CCOHS guide, op. cit., pp. 10–14; Western Australian code of practice, op. cit., pp. 5–13.

Figure 3.2 Hazard identification worksheet

Name of organization: The Green Family 24-Hour Supermarket

Information collected by: Susan Green – Supermarket Manager

Date: 2 April 2003

Task and location	Hazards	People affected	How often	Comments
Handling dissatisfied customers at front counter	Verbal abuse and physical violence from customers	Counter staff and customers who may be nearby	From time to time	
Handling drunken customers from pub next door	Verbal abuse and physical violence from customers	As above	Sometimes around pub closing time	
Maintaining rosters and managing customer service staff	Customer service too slow, resulting in unreasonable pressure on staff and irritated customers	Counter staff and customers waiting for service	Peak times	Need to move staff to the front counter when an employee is off sick
One person rostered at night	Robbery	Night-shift employees	After dark	Need to look at this
Handling cash at the counter	Robbery	All employees and customers who may be there	All times	Check cash handling and alert procedures
Handling cash in the office	Robbery	As above	Especially at quiet times	Need to review procedures
Unloading new stock in truck bay	Robbery of valuable goods, such as cigarettes	Employees in truck bay and truck drivers	Stock delivery times	New emergency help button has been installed
Shop-lifting	Physical violence if offenders are caught in the act	Employee who apprehends offender	At irregular times	

This form covers all employees and customers who may be affected by work in the supermarket.

Source: adapted from Western Australian code of practice, 1999, op. cit., p. 10.
Reproduced courtesy of the WorkSafe Western Austrialia Commission (www.safetyline.wa.gov.au).

well documented and are listed in box 3.2. It is important for an assessor to identify whether any of these established risk factors, or hazards, are present in the working environment and to identify situations where there is a potential for violence. These risk factors are not mutually exclusive. In certain occupations or sectors, a number of them may exist in combination.

- *Employees in high-risk situations:*[6] Many of the guidelines recommend that as part of the risk assessment the assessor identify those jobs, locations and specific employee groups with the greatest risk of violence. A number of occupational groups are identified as being at "greater risk" of Type 1 and Type 2 workplace violence. Some of these groups are described in box 3.2, while others include enforcement officers, security guards, taxi drivers, bar tenders and petrol pump attendants. It is important to note that these occupational groups are at greater risk primarily because their work involves multiple risk factors. Taxi drivers, for example, work alone but they are also in contact with the public, often carry valuables in the form of cash, and may encounter people in distress. That being said, it is still important for an assessor to identify the risk factors and hazards within the working environment and those employee groups who are at an increased risk of violence as a result of these factors/hazards. The presence of a single risk factor does not necessarily indicate that an employee group is at risk of violence. However, the presence of multiple risk factors, or a history of violence, should alert an employer to the increased potential for workplace violence.[7]

- *Trends in the industry:*[8] Another interesting form of information can come from other organizations within the same industry. Assessors can gain insight into the potential for violence in their own working environment by identifying the history or trend of violence in similar places of employment.

- *Legislative requirements:*[9] Guidelines often suggest that assessors contact legislative authorities to determine if any specific legislation regarding the prevention of workplace violence applies to their workplace. It is important for all assessors to understand the legal requirements within their country or jurisdiction.

- *Policies, procedures and systems that already exist to eliminate or minimize the risk of workplace violence:*[10] It is often suggested that an assessor identify and assess the effectiveness of any policies, procedures and/or systems that already exist within their organization to combat violence, including actions employees take to confront it. For example, an assessor may examine the effectiveness of existing security systems and devices and the need for improved security measures, or the success of policies to prevent Type 3 violence.

---

[6] OSHA health care guidelines, op. cit., pp. 3–4; Western Australian code of practice, op. cit., pp. 5–13.

[7] OSHA late-night retail guide, op. cit., pp. 3–4.

[8] Perrone, op. cit., pp. 78–80; WCBBC guide, op. cit., p. 10; CCOHS guide, op. cit., pp. 10–14.

[9] CCOHS guide, op. cit., pp. 10–14.

[10] Ishmael with Alemoru, op. cit., pp. 151–154; Perrone, op. cit., p. 79.

Box 3.2   What factors increase the risk of workplace violence?

Certain work processes, situations and interactions can put people at risk from workplace violence:

- working with the public;
- handling money, valuables or prescription drugs (e.g. cashiers, bank and post office staff, pharmacists);
- carrying out inspection of enforcement duties (e.g. government employees);
- providing service, care, advice or education (e.g. health care staff, social workers, teachers);
- working with unstable or volatile persons (e.g. health care, social services or criminal justice system employees);
- working in premises where alcohol is served (e.g. food and beverage staff);
- working alone or in small numbers (e.g. store clerks, real-estate agents);
- working in community-based settings (e.g. home visitors);
- having a mobile workplace (e.g. taxicab);
- working during periods of intense organizational change (e.g. strikes, downsizing).

Certain occupational groups tend to be more at risk from workplace violence:

- health care employees;
- prison officials;
- social services employees;
- teachers;
- municipal housing inspectors;
- public works employees;
- retail employees.

Risk of violence may be greater at certain times of the day, night or year:

- the late hours of the night or early hours of the morning;
- specific times of the day, days of the week or month:
  - tax return season;
  - overdue utility bill cut-off dates;
  - Christmas season in the retail market when demand for service is higher;
  - Friday or Saturday nights in establishments that serve alcohol;
  - pay days;
- in times of certain business or organizational activities that may increase stress, such as:
  - report cards or parent interviews;
  - performance appraisals;
  - contract negotiations.

continued

Violence among workers and managers may be linked to the work climate and job stress. Signs of a troubled or at-risk work environment that could lead to worker-on-worker violence include:

- chronic labour–management disputes;
- frequent grievances filed by employees (or a marked reduction in the number of grievances if employees don't believe that the system works);
- an extraordinary number of workers' compensation claims (especially for psychological illness or mental stress);
- understaffing or excessive demands for overtime;
- a high number of "stressed-out" workers;
- limited flexibility in how workers perform their jobs;
- pending or rumoured layoffs or "downsizing";
- significant changes in job responsibilities or workload;
- an authoritarian management style;
- competition for scarce resources.

Risk of violence may be greater because of the geographic location of the workplace:

- near buildings or businesses that are at risk of violent crime, e.g. bars, banks or certain social service agencies;
- in a location likely to be accidentally visited by violent, criminal, intoxicated or drugged persons;
- in high crime or dense manufacturing areas;
- isolated from other buildings or structures.

Source: adapted from CCOHS guide, 1999, op. cit., pp. 5–6.

These categories, although not exhaustive, illustrate the range of information that can be collected in the process of conducting a risk assessment. Please note that it is not always desirable, nor is it necessary, to collect all the information described above. Depending on the size of the organization and the nature of the business, different types of information will be more or less helpful. It is important to collect enough information to design an effective, targeted prevention strategy, while not collecting so much information as to inundate the assessor. The next section describes the different sources and methods through which this information can be collected.

Methods and sources

The information that is compiled when conducting a workplace violence risk assessment can be collected in a number of ways and from a number of sources. Based on a review of the existing guidelines in this area, there appear to be four primary sources of risk-assessment data. These sources include:

Figure 3.3 Conducting a risk assessment: Information sources and methods

Source	Possible methods	Information that can be collected
Employees	• Formal discussions (e.g. interviews, focus groups) • Informal discussions • Surveys	**Past incidents of violence:** employees can comment on whether they have ever experienced incidents of workplace violence, the nature of these incidents, and the potential for future incidents **Environmental and organizational features that put employees at risk:** employees can help identify hazards in their working environments **Employees in high-risk situations:** employees can help identify which jobs, locations and employee groups are at greatest risk of violence **Policies, procedures and systems that already exist to eliminate or minimize the risk of violence:** employees can comment on the effectiveness of existing policies, procedures or systems and suggest other interventions to prevent violence
Incident reports and relevant records	• Compiling and reading relevant reports/records • Examples may include: accident reports, safety and medical records, workers' compensation claims, grievances	**Past incidents of violence:** by reviewing these documents assessors can identify and analyse documented accounts of workplace violence (focus on last two or three years) Note: finding few documented cases does not mean that violence does not occur since incidents are often under-reported **Environmental and organizational features that put employees at risk:** by reviewing past incidents of violence, assessors can identify patterns/trends with regard to hazards **Employees in high-risk situations:** by reviewing past incidents of violence, assessors can determine whether certain jobs, locations or employee groups are at greater risk of violence *continued*

Working environment	• Workplace inspection • Security analysis	**Environmental and organizational features that put employees at risk:** through an inspection of the workplace, assessors can identify hazards or situations within the working environment and surrounding area that put workers at risk, e.g. groups who are understaffed **Employees in high-risk situations:** through an inspection of the workplace, assessors may be able to identify employees or work groups who are at an increased risk of violence **Policies, procedures and systems that already exist to eliminate or minimize the risk of violence:** one of the main goals of such an inspection is to assess the effectiveness of any existing security systems and devices, and the need for improved security measures
External businesses, groups and agencies	• Formal or informal discussions • Short survey • Letter	**Industry trends:** through communications with these external groups, assessors will be able to determine whether other businesses in the same industry and/or area have experienced incidents of workplace violence **Environmental and organizational features that put employees at risk:** through these communications, assessors will understand the circumstances that surround incidents of violence in similar organizations and, in the process, better understand the hazards which may exist in their organization **Legislative requirements:** by contacting governmental organizations, assessors will learn of relevant legal requirements regarding workplace violence

- **employees** (including union representatives);
- **incident reports and relevant records** (i.e. archival data);
- **the working environment;**
- **external businesses, groups and agencies** (e.g. local businesses, businesses in the same industry, trade associations, community groups, government organizations).

Figure 3.3 summarizes the types of risk-assessment information typically collected from each of these sources, as well as common collection methods.

Box 3.3   Hazard assessment

A hazard assessment is a method of identifying, analysing and documenting workplace hazards. Assessing workplace violence hazards involves some of the same tools used to document any other workplace safety or health problem. These include checklists and surveys, investigating incidents and reviewing available records.

1.   **Inspect the workplace** – A workplace violence inspection checklist can be used as part of a safety and health inspection or safety audit. While inspecting for workplace violence risk factors, review the physical facility and note the presence or absence of security measures. Local law enforcement officials may also be able to conduct a security audit or provide information about their experiences with crime in the area.

2.   **Conduct a survey** – The most important source of information on workplace hazards is workers. In fact, workers may be the only source of information on workplace violence hazards since management may not document incidents (or near misses). In addition, conducting regular surveys may also enable the local union to evaluate workplace violence prevention measures.

Information can be collected either through a written questionnaire distributed to workers or through one-to-one personal interviews. A written survey may be appropriate if the union wants personal or sensitive information. For example, a worker may be reluctant to voice to a union representative fears about a co-worker, but may be more willing to describe the problem in an anonymous questionnaire. Alternatively, a one-to-one interview is a good technique for organizing as it gets people talking about their jobs and working conditions. Oral surveys are also a way to involve workers who do not read well.

3.   **Analyse safety records** – By reviewing records of prior instances of workplace violence, local unions may be able to identify factors that contributed to the incident. Some of these documents must be requested from the employer. Others (for example, medical records or workers' compensation records) may require permission from the affected worker. Sensitive or confidential information may not be necessary to analyse the incidents; a summary of the information that includes at least the nature of the injury and type of treatment needed may be sufficient.

Source: adapted from AFSCME guide, 1998, op. cit., Ch. 3.

Both the AFSCME guide and the CCOHS guide describe the key steps involved in a risk or hazard assessment. Excerpts are taken from these two guides in boxes 3.3 and 3.4. These descriptions illustrate well the range of methods and sources that can be employed in such an assessment process.

Although these excerpts from the AFSCME and CCOHS guides target primarily the risks and hazards associated with Type 1 and Type 2 violence, these same methods and sources can uncover the risks and hazards associated

Box 3.4   Conducting a workplace violence risk assessment

Evaluate the history of violence in your own place of employment

Ask employees about their experiences, and whether they are concerned for themselves or others:

- Educate staff to increase their awareness of violence issues and to help them recognize incidents or situations which should be reported
- Emphasize that perceived or real threats of violence, near-misses and actual incidents of physical violence are all important
- Survey every employee
- Use interviews, a short questionnaire or a checklist
- Survey all shifts if you have more than one shift. Analyse the results separately, as trends may vary
- Use small discussion groups to generate more ideas
- Share the results of your review. This knowledge may prompt the identification of other relevant situations or incidents

Review any incidents of violence by consulting:

- Existing incident reports
- First aid records
- Health and safety committee records

Determine whether your workplace has any of the identified risk factors associated with violence:

- Work processes, situations or interactions (working alone, working with the public, handling cash)
- Occupational groups
- Time of the day, night or year
- Geographic location

Conduct a visual inspection of your workplace and the work being carried out, including:

- Workplace design and layout
- Administrative practices (e.g. visitor policy)
- Work practices

Evaluate the history of violence in similar places of employment

You may use one or more of the following approaches:

- Obtain information and advice from your insurer, regional or national insurance associations, your workers' compensation board, your occupational health and safety enforcement agency, your local police department, your union office
- Seek advice from a local security expert
- Review relevant publications, including industry-specific journals
- Contact your regional or national safety councils
- Contact your state, provincial or equivalent crime-prevention associations
- Contact your professional association or industry organization
- Collect newspaper or magazine clippings relating to violence in your industry

Contact legislative authorities to determine if specific legislation regarding workplace violence prevention applies to your workplace

Source: adapted from CCOHS guide, 2001, op. cit., pp. 10–12.

with Type 3 violence. Talking to employees and examining the work environment will probably yield the most relevant information associated with Type 3 violence. For example, surveying employees not only for violent incidents from the outside, but also from fellow workers would provide useful data (the Workplace Aggression Research Questionnaire, reproduced in figure 3.6 on page 42, is an example of such a survey). Also, scanning the working environment for those stressors known to be associated with Type 3 violence (e.g. under-staffing, excessive demands for overtime, authoritarian management style, excessive stress, etc.) would yield helpful information in identifying the risks associated with worker-on-worker violence.

Much of what has been described so far regarding the general approach to risk assessment is relevant to enterprises and workplaces of any type or size. There are, however, obvious reasons why the complexity and scale of this assessment is likely to increase or decrease in direct relation to the size of an enterprise. A good illustration of how the complexity can increase with size can be found in the United States Office of Personnel Management (OPM) guide, which is intended to provide advice to agency planners throughout the United States federal bureaucracy. The nature of the threats to the safety and security of the thousands of workers within that bureaucracy are clearly extremely diverse, ranging from terrorist attacks of the type that took a horrendous toll of life in Oklahoma City in 1995, to bullying and other inappropriate behaviours that cause fright to employees.[11]

Similarly, there are illustrations of how the complexity and scale of a risk assessment can decrease with the size of the enterprise. For example, the Workers' Compensation Board of British Columbia has developed a short method of conducting a risk assessment, as presented in box 3.5. It is important to note that this approach focuses on collecting information from employees and, as such, does not incorporate other potentially relevant data sources and methods, most notably a workplace inspection.

Small businesses can also contact local universities or colleges for help in conducting risk assessments.[12] Faculty members and students are often interested in gaining practical experience of this nature, and as such may be willing to accept less financial compensation. Departments with knowledge in the area of risk assessment include business, sociology, psychology and health-related disciplines.

Organizing and summarizing results

Having conducted a risk assessment of the type just described, it is very important to organize and review the results of this assessment in a way that facilitates the preparation of a workplace violence prevention programme. As set out at the beginning of this chapter, two basic questions need to be answered

[11] OPM guide, op. cit., foreword.

[12] J. Kinney: *Violence at work: How to make your company safe for employees and customers* (Englewood Cliffs, NJ, Prentice Hall, 1995), pp. 143–144.

Box 3.5   Short method of conducting a risk assessment

Here is a simple and effective way of conducting a risk assessment in organizations of all sizes.

- If your company is small, include all the employees.
- Larger organizations should gather as many employees as possible; ensure that at least one from every site, section and shift is present. Gather groups by division or job description, or include a representative from each. It is essential to involve the safety committee.
- Get the group to discuss the following three questions, asking each person to answer in turn.
  1. What violence have you been exposed to on this job?
  2. Do you know of any violence that has happened to others in similar jobs?
  3. What violence-related concerns do you have about this job?
- In a very large organization, you may want to supplement this process by sending all employees a form listing the three questions. The forms can be anonymous, but make sure employees list their job types, shifts and location (for example, "filing clerk, afternoon shift, Surrey office").
- List the answers on a chalkboard or a large sheet of paper. This should establish a comprehensive summary of the real and perceived risks.
- Many firms find it advantageous to include staff in establishing procedures for eliminating or minimizing risk. In any case, written procedures for the training of workers must be developed.

Source: adapted from WCBBC guide, 2001, op., cit., p. 12.

---

through the risk-assessment process:

1. *What is the level and nature of risk within the working environment?*
2. *Are there any policies, procedures or systems already in existence within the organization that help to eliminate or minimize the risk of violence?*

With regard to the first question, if records reveal that there are only a few isolated, dissimilar incidents of workplace violence, and little risk of future violence, then there is probably a limited case for preventive action.[13] It may be that potentially violent interactions are being satisfactorily managed or contained, in which case any aspects of present practice that may be responsible for this lack of violence should be identified and maintained. Where no violence comes to light, it is recommended that the question of risk be periodically revisited through discussions with staff.[14] This said, there are very few

---

[13] Poyner and Warne, op. cit., p. 10.

[14] ibid., pp. 8–9.

situations where the risk of future violence is so low that the organization could not benefit from policies and/or programmes in this area.

If a review of records and assessment information reveals an existing problem with workplace violence, and/or the probability of future violence, then the focus turns to the nature of the risk and the effectiveness of existing policies, procedures and/or systems. It is at this point that the assessor(s) should revisit their framework and fill in any relevant summary templates or worksheets. What is most important is to be able to articulate:

- who is at risk within the enterprise;
- what type of violence they are at risk of, and the severity of that risk; and
- what hazards put them at risk (are they at risk at certain times or in certain situations – what are the triggers?).

Examples of risk-assessment tools

Many of the existing prevention guidelines in this area provide examples of tools that can be used when conducting a risk assessment (e.g. checklists, surveys, worksheets, forms, etc.). These tools illustrate how other organizations collect assessment information and provide concrete examples from which to work. Four examples of such tools are provided in this section. *These tools are intended as examples to learn from, and are not being advocated for use by the ILO.* While the details of these tools can always be held up to question, those presented here should provide a useful starting point for the assessment of risk.

1. **Hazard Identification Worksheet:**[15] The Western Australian code of practice contains a number of "hazard identification worksheets" that provide a simple and effective framework for recording information. A blank worksheet is included in this section (figure 3.4).

2. **Hazard Assessment and Control Checklist:**[16] The Berkeley guide includes a very comprehensive checklist to be used when conducting a "walk-around" inspection of a fixed workplace (a building). The checklist, which is reproduced in full in figure 3.5, is not confined to a single industry or occupation but can be readily adapted for use in any fixed workplace. A separate checklist has also been developed for employees working in the field, where the hazards may be different (the field checklist is not reproduced here).

3. **Worker Survey:**[17] The Berkeley guide also includes a worker survey to help organizations determine the conditions that place employees at risk of workplace violence. The survey asks about risk factors, training, general security issues, and personal experience with violence on the job. A sample form from this survey is reproduced in full here (figure 3.6).

---

[15] Western Australian code of practice, op. cit., p. 28.

[16] Berkeley guide, op. cit., pp. 63–70.

[17] ibid., pp. 89–92.

4. **Workplace Behaviour Inventory:** This questionnaire was developed by Joel Neuman and Loraleigh Keashly as a part of their ongoing research in the area of workplace aggression.[18] This questionnaire asks individual members of an organization to indicate whether they have experienced certain aggressive behaviours on the job over the previous year. (The Workplace Behaviour Inventory is reproduced in figure 3.7).

---

[18] J.H. Neuman and L. Keashly: *Development of a measure of workplace aggression and violence: The Workplace Aggression Research Questionnaire (WAR-Q)*, unpublished paper, 2002. © Joel H. Neuman and Loraleigh Keashly.

Figure 3.4   Hazard identification worksheet

Name of organization:

Information collected by:

Date:

Task and location	Hazards	People affected	How often	Comments

This form covers all employees, clients and visitors who may be affected by the work processes.

Source: adapted from Western Australian code of practice, 1999, op. cit., p. 28.
Reproduced courtesy of the WorkSafe Western Australian Commission (www.safetyline.wa.gov.au).

Figure 3.5   Hazard assessment and control checklist

This checklist can help your committee evaluate the workplace and job tasks to see what situations may place employees at risk of assault. It is not confined to a single industry or occupation but can be used for any workplace. Adapt the checklist to fit your own needs. It is very comprehensive and not every question will apply to you. If a question does not apply to your workplace, write "N/A" in the Notes column. Add any other questions you think are important.

This checklist is designed for inspecting a fixed workplace (a building). If employees work outdoors, in the field, on the road, in clients' homes, etc., the *Jobs in the field* checklist (not reproduced here) will be more appropriate.

RISK FACTORS FOR WORKPLACE VIOLENCE

Cal/OSHA and NIOSH have identified the following risk factors that may contribute to violence in the workplace. If you have one or more of these risk factors in your workplace, there may be a potential for violence.

	Yes	No	Notes/ Follow-up action
Do workers have contact with the public?			
Do they exchange money with the public?			
Do they work with, guard or transport valuable items like money, jewellery or other property?			
Do they work alone?			
Do they work late at night or during early morning hours?			
Is the workplace often understaffed?			
Is the workplace located in an area with a high rate of assaults?			
Do workers perform public safety functions that might put them in conflict with others?			
Do they ever perform duties that could upset people (deny benefits, turn off utilities, collect debts, confiscate property, terminate child custody, etc.)?			
Do they deal with people known or suspected to have a history of violence?			
Do any employees or supervisors have a history of assault, verbal abuse, harassment or other threatening behaviour?			
Other risk factors (please describe):			

INSPECTING WORK AREAS

Who is responsible for building security (insert name)? . . . .

Are workers told who is responsible for security (please circle)?   YES   NO

Your joint committee should now begin a "walk-around" inspection to identify potential security hazards. This inspection can tell you which hazards are already well controlled, and what control measures need to be added. If you wish, use the space on the last page of this survey to draw a diagram of the workplace.

Not all the following questions can be answered through simple observation. You may also need to talk to employees or investigate in other ways.

	All areas	Some areas	Few areas	No areas	Notes/Follow-up action
Is public access to the building controlled?					
Are floor plans posted showing building entrances, exits and location of security personnel?					
Are these floor plans visible only to staff, not to outsiders?					
Is other emergency information posted, such as phone numbers?					
Are there enough exits and routes of escape?					
Can exit doors be opened only from the inside, to prevent unauthorized entry?					
Is there adequate staffing for protection against assaults or other violence?					
Is there a "buddy system" when workers are in potentially dangerous situations?					
Are special security measures taken to protect people who work late at night (escorts, locked entrances, etc.)?					
Is there enough lighting to see clearly in indoor areas?					
Are there employee-only work areas separate from public areas?					
Is access to work areas only through a reception area?					
Are reception areas and work areas designed to prevent unauthorized entry?					
Are visitors or clients escorted to offices for appointments?					
Are authorized visitors to the building required to wear ID badges?					

Are name tags required for staff (omitting personal information such as home address and last name)?					
Are workers notified of past violent acts by particular clients, patients, etc.?					
Are there trained security personnel, accessible to workers in a timely manner?					
Do security personnel have sufficient authority to take all necessary action to ensure worker safety?					
Is there established liaison with local police?					
Are bullet-proof windows or similar barriers used when money is exchanged with the public?					
Are areas where money is exchanged visible to others who could help in an emergency (for example, can you see cash register areas from outside?)					
Is a limited amount of cash kept on hand, with appropriate signs posted?					
Could someone hear a worker who called for help?					
Can workers observe patients or clients in waiting areas?					
Do areas used for patient or client interviews allow co-workers to observe any problems?					
Are waiting areas and work areas free of objects that could be used as weapons?					
Are chairs and furniture secured to prevent use as weapons?					
Is furniture in waiting areas and work areas arranged to prevent entrapment of employees?					
Are patient or client waiting areas designed to maximize comfort and minimize stress?					
Are patients or clients in waiting areas clearly informed how to use the department's services so that they will not become frustrated?					
Are waiting times for patient or client services kept short to prevent frustration?					
Are private, locked restrooms (toilets) available to staff?					
Is there a secure place for employees to store personal belongings?					

INSPECTING EXTERIOR BUILDING AREAS			
	Yes	No	Notes/ Follow-up action
Do workers feel safe walking to and from the workplace?			
Are the entrances to the building clearly visible from the street?			
Is the area surrounding the building free of bushes or other hiding places?			
Are security personnel provided outside the building?			
Is video surveillance provided outside the building?			
Is there enough lighting to see clearly outside the building?			
Are all exterior walkways visible to security personnel?			

INSPECTING PARKING AREAS			
	Yes	No	Notes/ Follow-up action
Is there a nearby parking lot reserved for employees only?			
Is the parking lot attended or otherwise secured?			
Is the parking lot free of bushes or other hiding places?			
Is there enough lighting to see clearly in the parking lot and when walking to the building?			
Are security escorts available to employees walking to and from the parking lot?			

WORKPLACE DIAGRAM

If you wish, use this box to draw a diagram of the workplace. Mark the location of security hazards.

SECURITY MEASURES

For the hazards that your committee identified during the inspection, indicate whether each control measure listed below is in place or should be added. (Many of the measures listed here may not be necessary or appropriate in your workplace.)

Does the workplace have...	In place	Should add	N/A	Notes/Follow-up action
Physical barriers (plexiglass partitions, bullet-proof customer windows, etc.)?				
Security cameras or closed-circuit TV in high-risk areas?				
Panic buttons?				
Alarm systems?				
Metal detectors?				
X-ray machines?				
Door locks?				
Internal phone system to activate emergency assistance?				
Phones with an outside line programmed for 911?*				
Two-way radios, pagers, or cellular phones?				
Security mirrors (e.g. convex mirrors)?				
Secured entry (e.g. "buzzers")?				
Personal alarm devices?				
"Drop safes" to limit amount of cash on hand?				
Broken windows repaired promptly?				
Security devices, locks, etc., tested on a regular basis and repaired promptly when necessary?				

*The telephone number to call for emergencies in the United States.

COMMENTS

Source: extracted from Berkeley guide, 1997, op. cit. pp. 63–70.

Figure 3.6 Worker survey: Sample form

Checklist completed by: .... Date: ....

This survey can help determine what conditions in your job may place you at risk of workplace violence. You do not have to give your name. Answer the question or circle the appropriate answer. Skip any question that does not apply to you.

Date: .... Job title: .... ☐ Male ☐ Female

Employer: .... Department/work location: ....

RISK FACTORS FOR WORKPLACE VIOLENCE

	Yes (Y)	No (N)	Unsure (?)
Do you have contact with the public?			
Do you exchange money with the public?			
Do you work in a community-based setting (social service field workers, home health aides, gas and water utility workers, etc.)?			
Do you work with, guard or transport valuable items like money, jewellery, or other property?			
Do you work alone?			
Do you work late at night or during early morning hours?			
Is your workplace often understaffed?			
Is your workplace located in an area with a high rate of assaults?			
Do you perform public safety functions that might put you in conflict with others?			
Do you ever perform duties that could upset people (deny benefits, turn off utilities, collect debts, confiscate property, terminate child custody, etc.)?			
Do you deal with people known or suspected to have a history of violence?			
Do any of your co-workers or supervisors have a history of assault, verbal abuse, harassment, or other threatening behaviour?			
List any other conditions on your job that may increase the risk of workplace violence:			

YOUR SECURITY ON THE JOB

On a scale of 1 to 10, how concerned are you about your personal safety at work? (1=not concerned, 10=very concerned. Circle a number below.)

1	2	3	4	5	6	7	8	9	10

On a scale of 1 to 10, how prepared do you feel to handle a violent situation or threat at work? (1=not concerned, 10=very concerned. Circle a number below.)

1	2	3	4	5	6	7	8	9	10

What security improvements are needed at your workplace? (Check all that apply, add any others below)

❑ better lighting   ❑ secure areas to store personal valuables

❑ more security personnel   ❑ better communication between employer and employees

❑ safer parking lot   ❑ restricting public access to work areas

❑ safer restrooms (toilets)   ❑ more security devices (cameras, alarms, panic buttons, metal detectors, etc.)

Other: . . . .

. . . .

If you ever work in the field, are you given: (Check all that apply, explain below if you wish)

❑ a safe vehicle?   ❑ good information about the area?

❑ a cellular phone or radio?   ❑ timely assistance when you report a problem?

❑ a security contact person?

Comments: . . . .

. . . .

VIOLENCE PREVENTION POLICY

	Yes (Y)	No (N)	Unsure (?)
Is there a written violence prevention policy for your workplace?			
Have you ever seen a copy of the policy?			

Comments: . . . .

. . . .

INCIDENT REPORTING AND FOLLOW-UP			
	Yes (Y)	No (N)	Unsure (?)
Is the system for reporting threats and violent incidents clear to you?			
Are you encouraged to report threats and violent incidents without fear of reprisal?			
Are police and emergency services called immediately when an incident occurs?			
Is there a programme to provide support for employees who are victims of workplace violence?			

Comments: . . . .

. . . .

TRAINING			
	Yes (Y)	No (N)	Unsure (?)
Have you received training on the job about workplace violence?			
Are you trained at least once a year or when your job duties change?			
Is training adequate?			
Is training appropriate for the job that you do? (Is it tailored to your particular job duties?)			

Comments: . . . .

. . . .

Does the training include: (check all that apply; explain below if you wish)

❑ ways to prevent workplace violence?

❑ how to recognize warning signs of potential violence?

❑ ways to respond to hostile or threatening situations?

❑ use of the alarm systems and/or security devices?

❑ what to do in an emergency?

❑ specific information on the violence-prevention programme in your workplace?

Comments: . . . .

. . . .

INCIDENTS AT WORK

Have you ever been the victim of
a violent incident on the job?   ❏ Yes   ❏ No

If yes, please answer the following:

Date of incident: . . . .

Type of incident (describe): . . . .

. . . .

Were you injured?   ❏ Yes   ❏ No

If so, describe injuries: . . . .

Did you receive medical treatment?   ❏ Yes   ❏ No

If so, describe: . . . .

Did you report the incident?   ❏ Yes   ❏ No

Which term best describes the perpetrator?

❏ customer/client	❏ student	❏ other relative
❏ patient	❏ passenger	❏ stranger
❏ supervisor	❏ partner/spouse	❏ person in custody
❏ co-worker	❏ former partner/spouse	❏ animal
❏ robber/burglar	❏ other (please describe):	

YOUR OPINION

In your opinion, what steps could be taken to make your workplace safer?

. . . .

. . . .

. . . .

Name (optional): . . . . I would like more information: ❏ Yes   ❏ No

Source: extracted from Berkeley guide, 1997, op. cit. pp. 89–92.

© Labor Occupational Health Program, University of California at Berkeley.

Figure 3.7   Workplace behaviour inventory

We are interested in learning **whether or not you have experienced certain kinds of behaviours in your workplace** *over the past 12 months*. For each of the items listed in column A, please indicate *how often you have been subjected to such behaviour* (in column B) and *who was most responsible for doing this to you* (in column C). For example, if a co-worker has subjected you to bad jokes on a weekly basis, you would darken the circle for "weekly" in column B and then fill in the circle for "Co-worker" in column C (as demonstrated in the SAMPLE ITEM shown below). If more than one person has engaged in a behaviour towards you, just indicate the relationship of the one person who was *most responsible* for that particular behaviour. Please do NOT darken more than one circle in columns B or C.

For column C, please use the following definitions:

Superior: A direct supervisor or any other individual in the organization who holds a higher-level position than yours.

Co-worker: A person with whom you work who holds a position that is neither superior nor subordinate to yours.

Subordinate: A person who reports to you or an individual who holds a lower-level position than yours.

Customer: An individual for whom your organization provides a product or service (e.g. customer, patient, client).

Other: Any other individual not covered under the above-referenced categories.

Not applicable: Select this option if you have never experienced that particular behaviour at work.

SECTION I: WHAT WORKPLACE BEHAVIOURS HAVE YOU BEEN SUBJECTED TO?

	A	B	C
	Have you been subjected to any of the behaviours listed below in the past 12 months? Only consider those behaviours that have occurred in your workplace.	How often have you been subjected to this behaviour in your workplace over the past 12 months?	Who was most responsible for doing this to you?

	Never	Once	A few times	Several times	Monthly	Weekly	Daily		Not applicable	Superior	Co-worker	Subordinate	Customer	Other
Subjected to bad jokes SAMPLE ITEM	○	○	○	○	○	●	○		○	○	●	○	○	○
Been glared at in a hostile manner	○	○	○	○	○	○	○		○	○	○	○	○	○
Been excluded from work-related social gatherings	○	○	○	○	○	○	○		○	○	○	○	○	○
Had others storm out of the work area when you entered	○	○	○	○	○	○	○		○	○	○	○	○	○

Had others consistently arrive late for meetings that you called	○○○○○○	○○○○○○
Been sworn at in a hostile manner	○○○○○○	○○○○○○
Been subjected to negative comments about your religious beliefs	○○○○○○	○○○○○○
Been given the "silent treatment"	○○○○○○	○○○○○○
Not given the praise to which you felt entitled	○○○○○○	○○○○○○
Been treated in a rude and/or disrespectful manner	○○○○○○	○○○○○○
Had your personal property defaced, damaged or stolen	○○○○○○	○○○○○○
Had others fail to take action to protect you from harm	○○○○○○	○○○○○○
Been subjected to negative comments about a disability	○○○○○○	○○○○○○
Been subjected to obscene or hostile gestures	○○○○○○	○○○○○○
Had others refuse your requests for assistance	○○○○○○	○○○○○○
Had others fail to deny false rumours about you	○○○○○○	○○○○○○
Been given little or no feedback about your performance	○○○○○○	○○○○○○
Had others delay action on matters that were important to you	○○○○○○	○○○○○○
Been yelled at or shouted at in a hostile manner	○○○○○○	○○○○○○
Been subjected to negative comments about your intelligence or competence	○○○○○○	○○○○○○
Had others consistently fail to return your telephone calls and/or respond to your memos or e-mail	○○○○○○	○○○○○○
Had your contributions ignored by others	○○○○○○	○○○○○○
Had someone interfere with your work activities	○○○○○○	○○○○○○
Been subjected to mean pranks	○○○○○○	○○○○○○
Been lied to	○○○○○○	○○○○○○
Had others fail to give you information that you really needed	○○○○○○	○○○○○○
Been subjected to threats and/or harassment for "blowing the whistle" about activities at work	○○○○○○	○○○○○○
Had others fail to warn you about impending dangers	○○○○○○	○○○○○○
Been denied a rise or promotion without being given a valid reason	○○○○○○	○○○○○○
Had signs or notes left that embarrassed you	○○○○○○	○○○○○○
Been subjected to derogatory name calling	○○○○○○	○○○○○○
Been blamed for other people's mistakes	○○○○○○	○○○○○○
Been the target of rumours or gossip	○○○○○○	○○○○○○
Been shown little empathy/sympathy when you were having a tough time	○○○○○○	○○○○○○
Had co-workers fail to defend your plans or ideas to others	○○○○○○	○○○○○○
Been given unreasonable workloads or deadlines–more than others	○○○○○○	○○○○○○
Had others destroy or needlessly take resources that you needed to do your job	○○○○○○	○○○○○○
Been accused of deliberately making an error	○○○○○○	○○○○○○
Been subjected to unwanted attempts to touch, fondle, kiss or grab you	○○○○○○	○○○○○○
Been subjected to threats to reveal private or embarrassing information about you to others	○○○○○○	○○○○○○
Been subjected to temper tantrums when disagreeing with someone	○○○○○○	○○○○○○

Preventing and responding to violence at work

Been prevented from expressing yourself (e.g. interrupted when speaking)	○ ○ ○ ○ ○ ○ ○	○ ○ ○ ○ ○ ○
Had attempts made to turn other employees against you	○ ○ ○ ○ ○ ○ ○	○ ○ ○ ○ ○ ○
Had someone flaunt his/her status or treat you in a condescending manner	○ ○ ○ ○ ○ ○ ○	○ ○ ○ ○ ○ ○
Been subjected to excessively harsh criticism about your work	○ ○ ○ ○ ○ ○ ○	○ ○ ○ ○ ○ ○
Had someone else take credit for your work or ideas	○ ○ ○ ○ ○ ○ ○	○ ○ ○ ○ ○ ○
Been kicked, bitten or spat on	○ ○ ○ ○ ○ ○ ○	○ ○ ○ ○ ○ ○
Been criticized for non-work (personal) life and activities	○ ○ ○ ○ ○ ○ ○	○ ○ ○ ○ ○ ○
Been subjected to negative comments about your sexual orientation	○ ○ ○ ○ ○ ○ ○	○ ○ ○ ○ ○ ○
Been subjected to racist remarks	○ ○ ○ ○ ○ ○ ○	○ ○ ○ ○ ○ ○
Been reprimanded or "put down" in front of others	○ ○ ○ ○ ○ ○ ○	○ ○ ○ ○ ○ ○
Had someone hit you with an object	○ ○ ○ ○ ○ ○ ○	○ ○ ○ ○ ○ ○
Been subjected to ethnic or racial jokes or slurs	○ ○ ○ ○ ○ ○ ○	○ ○ ○ ○ ○ ○
Been told how to spend your personal time when not at work	○ ○ ○ ○ ○ ○ ○	○ ○ ○ ○ ○ ○
Been subjected to unwanted terms of endearment	○ ○ ○ ○ ○ ○ ○	○ ○ ○ ○ ○ ○
Been subjected to suggestive and/or offensive stories	○ ○ ○ ○ ○ ○ ○	○ ○ ○ ○ ○ ○
Been subjected to sexist remarks	○ ○ ○ ○ ○ ○ ○	○ ○ ○ ○ ○ ○
Been threatened with physical harm	○ ○ ○ ○ ○ ○ ○	○ ○ ○ ○ ○ ○
Been pushed, shoved, thrown or bumped into with unnecessary force	○ ○ ○ ○ ○ ○ ○	○ ○ ○ ○ ○ ○
Been raped or sexually assaulted	○ ○ ○ ○ ○ ○ ○	○ ○ ○ ○ ○ ○
Been assaulted with a weapon or other dangerous object	○ ○ ○ ○ ○ ○ ○	○ ○ ○ ○ ○ ○

In the spaces provided below, please list any "other" behaviours that you have experienced and then darken the circles to the right indicating the extent to which each has occurred and who was responsible.

Other:	○ ○ ○ ○ ○ ○ ○	○ ○ ○ ○ ○ ○
Other:	○ ○ ○ ○ ○ ○ ○	○ ○ ○ ○ ○ ○
Other:	○ ○ ○ ○ ○ ○ ○	○ ○ ○ ○ ○ ○

Overall, how much have these situations bothered you?	○	○	○	○
	not at all	a little	moderately	quite a lot

Is there any additional information or clarification that you believe would be helpful?

SECTION II: YOUR RESPONSE TO, AND ASSESSMENT OF, THE ABOVE-REFERENCED BEHAVIOURS

During the past 12 months, did you:	Yes	No
Report any of these experiences to a superior or union official?	O	O
Confront the person(s) involved in any of these behaviours?	O	O
File a formal complaint or grievance about any of these experiences?	O	O

Which of the following factors do you think may have contributed to all or any of the experiences you reported in section I?	Yes	No
Your gender	O	O
Your race	O	O
Your ethnic group	O	O
Your age	O	O
Your religion	O	O
Your political beliefs	O	O
Your health, illness or disability	O	O
Your sexual orientation	O	O
Your job level	O	O
Your own behaviour	O	O
The personality traits of others	O	O
Office politics	O	O
Your union affiliation	O	O
Stress	O	O

Other (please specify):

Source: J.H. Neuman and L. Keashly: *Development of a measure of workplace aggression and violence: The Workplace Aggression Research Questionnaire (WAR-Q)*, unpublished paper, 2002.
© Joel H. Neuman and Loraleigh Keashly

STEP 2 – DESIGN AND IMPLEMENT PREVENTIVE MEASURES

4

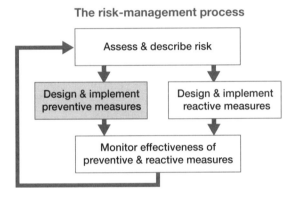

The risk-management process

Assess & describe risk

Design & implement preventive measures

Design & implement reactive measures

Monitor effectiveness of preventive & reactive measures

The purpose of designing and implementing preventive measures

The next step after assessing the degree of risk and identifying existing hazards within the working environment is to design/select and implement measures to address these hazards, and to eliminate or reduce the risk of workplace violence. Two basic questions need to be answered through this second step in the risk-management process:

1. *Which of the possible preventive measures will be most effective at addressing the specific hazards within the working environment, thereby eliminating or reducing the risk of workplace violence?* There will probably be a range of possible measures to choose from. Those individuals involved in this process need to work collaboratively to identify the combination of measures that will address the underlying issues in the most effective and efficient manner.

2. *How and when will the measures be implemented?* In order to ensure success, the measures need to be implemented in the appropriate sequence and in a way that facilitates the commitment and cooperation of staff. Furthermore, it is important that those employees responsible for implementation receive the training, guidance and support necessary.

The discussion that follows is centred around three key components of any systematic preventive strategy:

- Reporting procedures
- Risk-reduction measures
- Education and training

Reporting procedures

Once a problem with violence has been identified within an organization, it is commonly agreed that a formal system for reporting, recording and investigating incidents of violence should be initiated (assuming that one does not already exist).[1] There are three important arguments for developing such a system. First and foremost, there must be an avenue through which employees can report incidents of violence so that appropriate support can be provided, and any corrective action can be taken. Further, by recording what is perceived as "minor" incidents of violence an organization has the opportunity to take action and prevent any further escalation of violence. Lastly, the process of recording and classifying incidents of violence can help to further tailor and improve preventive measures by highlighting important patterns or trends.

The importance of reporting procedures is emphasized in many of the existing guidelines, including the OPM guide, which lists the development of reporting procedures among the essential steps in the planning process to deal with workplace violence.[2] This guide highlights a number of the key features characteristic of effective reporting systems:

- the reporting of *all* incidents, not just the most serious ones;
- the confidential nature of the process;
- the lack of any actual or perceived penalties associated with reporting incidents;
- management's support of the process and encouragement for reporting incidents;
- the quick, effective and consistent handling of reports. *Please note:* given that investigations of this nature can have legal ramifications, it is important that organizations determine who will investigate reports of violence (i.e. those with the required skills/experience) and what this process will look like before any incidents occur.[3]

---

[1] CCOHS guide, op. cit., pp. 18–20; A. Ishmael with B. Alemoru: *Harassment, bullying and violence at work: A practical guide to combating employee abuse* (London, The Industrial Society, 1999), pp. 52–53; WCBBC guide, op. cit., p. 14.

[2] OPM guide, op. cit., pp. 10–11.

[3] CCOHS guide, op. cit., pp. 18–19.

Reporting procedures, to be effective, require careful tailoring to the needs and circumstances of individual workplaces. For example, elaborate record-keeping and reporting may be required more in larger enterprises than in smaller ones. Many organizations choose to develop a simple form to facilitate the reporting of incidents. The sample incident form provided in figure 4.1 (overleaf) illustrates the information typically captured in such a form.

It is widely acknowledged that workers are often reluctant to report incidents of work-related violence owing to a lack of confidence in the process through which their report is received by management. There are a number of other reasons why people are reluctant to report incidents:

- many fear that involvement in a violent incident will be seen as their mishandling of the situation;
- others start to believe that the experience of violence is "just part of the job";
- some workers are already so upset by the experience that they do not want the added stress and attention that filing a report would bring;[4]
- others fear retaliation not only from the perpetrator but also from the leaders to whom they report, particularly when the leader is a "valued" employee; and
- some may believe that nothing will be done.[5]

In order to ensure that incidents of violence are actually reported, it is important that the reporting process is seen as fair and consistent, and that the act of reporting is part of the organizational culture (i.e. an accepted norm). That is, when a complaint is laid, an investigation occurs in a timely manner, everyone is kept informed, and the outcomes are seen as fair and consistent.

Risk-reduction measures

The goal of any workplace violence prevention strategy is to eliminate situations that may result in violence and to reduce the risk of injury or harm. Given the wide range of organizations and industries that are affected by workplace violence, there is a large number of different risk-reduction measures that can help organizations to accomplish this goal. Deciding on which measure(s) to implement will depend on the exact nature of the risk involved, as well as the characteristics of the organization in question (e.g. size, location). Further, this process of developing and deciding upon preventive measures to combat the problem of violence is best done through a participative process where employees are fully involved.

Most risk-reduction measures fall under one of the following broad categories:[6]

---

[4] UNISON guide, op. cit., pp. 8–9.

[5] L. Keashly and K. Jagatic: "By any other name: American perspectives on workplace bullying", in S. Einarsen et al. (eds.): *Bullying and emotional abuse in the workplace: International perspectives on research and practice* (London, Taylor & Francis, 2003).

[6] OSHA late-night retail guide, op. cit., pp. 6–7; S. Perrone: *Violence in the workplace*, Research and Public Policy Series, No. 22 (Canberra, Australian Institute of Criminology, 1999), pp. 81–84; AFSCME guide, op. cit., Ch. 4; Berkeley guide, op. cit., pp. 24–25.

Figure 4.1   Sample reporting form

VIOLENCE INCIDENT REPORT FORM

Date of report: . . . .

Date of incident (day/month/year): . . . . Time of incident: . . . .

Employee

Name: . . . .

Work address: . . . .

Job/position: . . . .   Department/section: . . . .

Age: . . . .   ❑ Male   ❑ Female

What were you doing at the time of the incident? . . . .

. . . .

Offender(s)

Name(s): . . . .

Work address(es): . . . .

Age: . . . .   ❑ Male   ❑ Female

Description: . . . .

Relationship between employee and offender (if any):

❑ co-worker ❑ patient ❑ client ❑ student ❑ member of public ❑ other (specify):

. . . .

Other details (e.g. use of drugs or alcohol, possession of a weapon): . . . .

. . . .

Apparent motive: . . . .

Witness(es)

Names and addresses: . . . .

. . . .

. . . .

continued

Details of the incident

Type of incident (physical injury, verbal abuse, threatening behaviour, verbal threat, written threat, damage to personal/other property): . . . .
. . . .
. . . .

Location of incident (attach a sketch if possible): . . . .
. . . .
. . . .

Outcome (assailant apprehended, police called, medical assistance required, first-aid treatment required, time lost, emotional shock or distress, legal action initiated):
. . . .
. . . .

Other relevant information (to be completed as appropriate): . . . .
. . . .
. . . .

Possible contributing factors: . . . .
. . . .
. . . .

Relevant events which preceded the incident: . . . .
. . . .
. . . .

Suggested preventive/remedial actions: . . . .
. . . .
. . . .

Submit this report to:

Name: . . . .

Title: . . . .

Location: . . . .

Source: adapted from CCOHS guide, 1999, op. cit., pp. 162–163.

1. **Engineering controls:** These controls either remove the hazard from the workplace or create a barrier between the worker and the hazard by manipulating the physical design of the working environment and/or surrounding area.[7] Examples include: installing security equipment; controlled access to entrances; providing mobile phones for workers in the field; and enhancing the design of waiting rooms.

2. **Work practice and administrative controls:** These controls change the way employees perform their work in order to reduce the likelihood of violence.[8] Examples include: prohibiting employees from working alone; keeping only a minimal amount of money on hand; training employees in handling difficult clients; and ensuring adequate staffing levels.

How does an organization choose which risk-reduction or control measure(s) to implement? One approach is to tailor the prevention programme to the types of violence identified as being of highest risk within a given enterprise. The three types of violence, suggested by researchers at the California Department of Industrial Relations, were discussed earlier (i.e. violence from criminal intruders, from clients or customers, and from internal employees).[9] The California researchers propose that each category of violence requires specific, but different, responses. A rich choice exists in the risk-reduction measures that can be adopted for each type of violence based not only on the original research, and the various refinements which have been made to this research,[10] but also on the practical experience gained in specific workplaces with policies that have been implemented in the field. It must be remembered, however, that in many workplaces it is likely that more than one category of violence may require attention. In this chapter, examples are provided of risk-reduction measures which are linked to each of the three principal categories of violence that have been identified.

Addressing Type 1 risk factors

Background: Type 1 scenarios include incidents involving agents with no legitimate nexus to the organization or workplace, e.g. intruders bent upon the commission of a criminal activity:

> To many people, Type 1 workplace violence appears to be part of society's "crime" problem, and not a workplace safety and health problem at all. Under this view, the workplace is an "innocent bystander" and the solution to the problem involves societal changes, not occupational safety and health principles.

---

[7] Berkeley guide, op. cit., p. 24.

[8] AFSCME guide, op. cit., Ch. 4.

[9] Cal/OSHA guide, op. cit.

[10] H. Standing and D. Nicolini: *Review of workplace violence* (London, HSE, 1997). The Cal/OSHA model has been both adopted and adapted progressively by a succession of researchers and policy-makers. For instance, the OSHA guide added a fourth type of violence (violence resulting from personal relationships) and the revised Tavistock model (Tavistock Institute) acknowledges and bears a strong relationship to the Cal/OSHA model but elaborates further upon both the capacity and responsibility of organizations to act proactively to prevent workplace violence.

The ultimate solution to Type 1 events may indeed involve societal changes, but until such changes occur it is still the employer's legal responsibility ... to provide a safe and healthful place of employment for their employees.

Employers with employees who are known to be at risk for Type 1 events are required to address workplace security hazards to satisfy the regulatory requirement of establishing, implementing and maintaining an effective Injury and Illness Prevention (IIP) Program.[11]

The Tavistock Institute argues that beyond security measures, organizations at risk of Type 1 violence need to establish reporting and diffusion mechanisms, as well as support programmes to help victims cope with the aftermath of violent incidents.[12]

Practical examples: A good illustration of a guideline which seeks to deal principally with workplace violence involving criminal intruders is the OSHA-formulated violence prevention programme for late-night retail establishments.[13] Experience suggests that in such establishments (which tend to be small in size), and especially those in the United States, the major risk of death or serious injury to employees comes from robbery-related violence by criminals armed with guns. Thus an effective violence prevention programme would include, but not be limited to, steps to reduce the risk of robbery. The workplace violence prevention tools likely to achieve this objective include specific engineering controls, as well as work practice controls. As the OSHA document on this topic stresses that no single control will protect employees, the organization should use a combination of controls to address the hazards identified in the risk assessment in order to provide effective deterrents to violence.[14]

The OSHA document goes on to explain how the risk of robbery may be reduced by increasing the effort that the offender must expend through measures such as controlling access to the establishment; increasing the risk of the offender being identified and apprehended through surveillance mechanisms; and reducing the rewards to the offender through the removal or securing of items like cash. The document also offers comprehensive advice regarding the types of physical and associated measures that should be considered as part of this hazard-reduction process (boxes 4.1 and 4.2).

In addition to these very specific recommendations, the OSHA document provides examples of ways in which work practices and administrative procedures can help prevent incidents of workplace violence in late-night retail establishments.[15]

---

[11] Cal/OSHA guide, op. cit., p. 9.

[12] Standing and Nicolini, op. cit.

[13] OSHA late-night retail guide, op. cit.

[14] ibid., p. 6.

[15] This guide also offers a general framework to help with the development of an effective violence prevention programme, including the establishment of standard operating procedures to follow after a violent incident; the provision of training/education to ensure that all staff are aware of potential security hazards and procedures for personal protection; and the creation of a good record-keeping system.

Box 4.1 Retail establishments: Engineering controls and workplace adaptation

Engineering controls remove the hazard from the workplace or create a barrier between the worker and the hazard. The following physical changes in the workplace can help reduce violence-related risks or hazards in retail establishments:

Improve visibility, as this is important in preventing robbery in two respects. First, employees should be able to see their surroundings and, second, persons outside the store, including police on patrol, should be able to see into the store. Employees in the store should have an unobstructed view of the street, clear of shrubbery, trees or any form of clutter that a criminal could use to hide. Signs located in windows should be either low or high to allow good visibility into the store. The customer service and cash register areas should be visible from outside the establishment. Shelves should be low enough to assure good visibility throughout the store. Convex mirrors, two-way mirrors and an elevated vantage point can give employees a more complete view of their surroundings.

Maintain adequate lighting within and outside the establishment to make the store less appealing to a potential robber by making detection more likely. The parking area and the approach to the retail establishment should be well lit during night-time hours of operation. Exterior illumination may need upgrading in order to allow employees to see what is occurring outside the store.

Use fences and other structures to direct the flow of customer traffic to areas of greater visibility.

Use drop safes to limit the availability of cash to robbers. Employers using drop safes can post signs stating that the amount of cash on hand is limited.

Install video surveillance equipment and closed circuit television (CCTV) to deter robberies by increasing the risk of identification. This may include interactive video equipment. The video recorder for the CCTV should be secure and out of sight. Posting signs that surveillance equipment is in use and placing the equipment near the cash register may increase the effectiveness of the deterrence.

Put height markers on exit doors to help witnesses provide more complete descriptions of assailants.

Use door detectors to alert employees when persons enter the store.

Control access to the store with door buzzers.

Use silent and personal alarms to notify police or management in the event of a problem. To avoid angering a robber, however, an employee may need to wait until the assailant has left before triggering an alarm.

Install physical barriers such as bullet-resistant enclosures with pass-through windows between customer and employees to protect employees from assaults and weapons in locations with a history of robberies or assaults and located in high-crime areas.

Source: adapted from OSHA late-night retail guide, 1998, op. cit., pp. 6–7.

Box 4.2 Retail establishments: Administrative and work practice controls

Integrate violence prevention activities into daily procedures, such as checking lighting, locks and security cameras, to help maintain worksite readiness.

Keep a minimal amount of cash in each register (e.g. $50 or less), especially during evening and late-night hours of operation. In some businesses, transactions with large bills (over $20) can be prohibited. In situations where this is not practical because of frequent transactions in excess of $20, cash levels should be as low as is practical. Employees should not carry business receipts on their person unless it is absolutely necessary.

Adopt proper emergency procedures for employees to use in case of a robbery or security breach.

Establish systems of communication in the event of emergencies. Employees should have access to working telephones in each work area, and emergency telephone numbers should be posted by the phones.

Adopt procedures for the correct use of physical barriers, such as enclosures and pass-through windows.

Increase staffing levels at night at stores with a history of robbery or assaults and located in high-crime areas. It is important that clerks be clearly visible to patrons.

Lock doors used for deliveries and disposal of garbage when not in use. Also, do not unlock delivery doors until the delivery person identifies himself or herself. Take care not to block emergency exits – doors must open from the inside without a key to allow persons to exit in case of fire or other emergency.

Establish rules to ensure that employees can walk to garbage areas and outdoor freezers or refrigerators without increasing their risk of assault. The key is for employees to have good visibility, thereby eliminating potential hiding places for assailants near these areas. In some locations, taking trash out or going to outside freezers during daylight may be safer than doing so at night.

Keep doors locked before business officially opens and after closing time. Establish procedures to assure the security of employees who open and close the business, when staffing levels may be low. In addition, the day's business receipts may be a prime robbery target at store closing.

Limit or restrict areas of customer access, reduce the hours of operation, or close portions of the store to limit risk.

Adopt safety procedures and policies for off-site work, such as deliveries.

Administrative controls are effective only if they are followed and used properly. Regular monitoring helps ensure that employees continue to use proper work practices. Giving periodic, constructive feedback to employees helps to ensure that they understand these procedures and their importance.

Source: adapted from OSHA late-night retail guide, 1998, op. cit., pp. 7–8.

> ### Box 4.3   Retail solutions
>
> Shops can take measures to tackle the problems of violence against staff, and many have.
>
> Staff at a Safeway store in Taunton, Somerset, United Kingdom, used to face a barrage of abuse and threats from people around their store.
>
> "We were having a lot of problems from drunks and drug addicts hanging around the store", says a USDAW shop steward. "Staff were being verbally abused and threatened – one security guard even had a knife pointed in his face. Staff cars were damaged and broken into and there was a big problem with vandalism."
>
> Having asked their management to do something about the problem, with no success, the union branch approached the police for advice and persuaded the local press to run a story on the problem.
>
> When they talked to management again, they had more luck. Cameras and lighting were installed and a better relationship with the local police was established. The result was a marked fall in incidents.
>
> Source: adapted from Gallagher, 1999, op. cit., p. 21.

The engineering, administrative and work practice controls suggested by the OSHA, and presented in boxes 4.1 and 4.2, provide quite a comprehensive list of recommended ways to respond to workplace violence in late-night retail establishments. Although this list of possible risk-reduction measures may appear long, only selected measures will be implemented depending on the nature of the risk involved. As illustrated in box 4.3, action to curb violence need not be expensive or complicated. Simple measures can often act to alleviate the risk of violence and to safeguard staff.

Addressing Type 2 risk factors

Background: Type 2 scenarios include incidents involving agents who are the recipients of some service provided by the organization, e.g. current or former client, patient, customer. According to the researchers of the California Department of Industrial Relations in the United States, workplace design features can provide an important source of preventive action:

> Employers concerned with Type 2 events need to be aware that the control of physical access through workplace design is also an important preventive measure. This can include controlling access into and out of the workplace and freedom of movement within the workplace, in addition to placing barriers between clients and service providers. Escape routes can also be a critical component of workplace design. In certain situations, the installation of alarm systems or "panic buttons" may be an appropriate back-up measure. Establishing a "buddy" system to be used in specified

emergency situations is often advisable as well. The presence of security personnel should also be considered where appropriate.[16]

It has been suggested that organizations have a much broader range of action with respect to Type 2 incidents than with Type 1 incidents, since they can influence some important aspects of the context in which these incidents occur.[17] For example, many of the incidents in this category refer to situations where the agent is not satisfied with the service provided. In this scenario, organizations can minimize the risk of violence by implementing changes to the way service is provided, or by training employees in handling difficult clients.

Practical examples: A good illustration of how to prevent incidents involving clients or customers can be found in recent guidelines developed by the airline industry and aimed at addressing the problem of disruptive or unruly passengers. Violence in the sky, or "air rage", as it has been more typically described, has become both a more visible and frequently reported occurrence.[18] International regulatory authorities, as well as airline companies, flight crew unions and other bodies, are now taking a range of steps to prevent and manage unruly passenger behaviour.[19] The International Air Transport Association (IATA), for example, has produced a comprehensive and practical action guide on this subject for use by its membership, which includes most of the world's major airlines.[20] The IATA guide, which uses a risk-management framework, notes that it is not possible to predict human behaviour and that solutions to this problem need to be tailored to individual circumstances. The objective of the IATA guide is "not to offer a turnkey solution" but rather to propose ways and techniques of preventing aggressive behaviour by passengers based on successful measures used by airlines operating in diverse cultural settings.[21]

The description provided in the IATA guide of the preventive measures that can be adopted reflects a clear recognition by the airline industry that "air rage" can result from a combination of factors, including the actions of the airlines themselves handling their clients from the moment of check-in to the completion of a flight. There are many ways in which airline practices and procedures may be modified in order to prevent or minimize the risk of "air rage" escalating into an incident affecting the safety of a flight. Some of these practices and procedures are discussed in box 4.4.

---

[16] Cal/OSHA guide, op. cit., p. 11.

[17] Standing and Nicolini, op. cit., pp. 33–37.

[18] Gallagher, op. cit., p. 19.

[19] Prompted by pressure groups such as the Skyrage Foundation, as well as by industry unions and groups, the United States Congress held hearings on the issue in 1997. The Skyrage Foundation's objective is to reduce occurrences of in-flight disruption and violence towards crew members and passengers. See http://www.skyrage.org.

[20] IATA: *Guidelines for handling disruptive/unruly passengers* (Geneva, 1998) (hereafter IATA guide). This guide contains substantial advice regarding other essential components of a workplace violence prevention programme, including reporting and evaluation procedures, training and education requirements, and methods of handling critical incidents.

[21] ibid., foreword. See also International Transport Workers' Federation (ITF), Civil Aviation Section: *Air rage: The prevention and management of disruptive passenger behaviour*, Safety in Practice, No. 1 (London, 2000); http://www.itf.org.uk.

Box 4.4   Violence prevention in the airline industry

Disruptive/unruly behaviour in the airline industry is first of all a safety issue. It also puts great mental strain on the passengers and employees involved. Prevention of (escalated) disruptive behaviour should therefore be the focus of an airline's approach. Dealing firmly and legally with disruptive behaviour may serve as a deterrent, but an airline cannot rely on its effect. In many disruptive incidents, passengers behave irrationally and will not calculate the consequences of their behaviour.

The study of disruptive behaviour shows that often a series of events *builds up* to the disruptive behaviour and early signs of potential disruptive behaviour can be observed.

The focus of company policy should be first on prevention by acting on these early signs, rather than dealing exclusively with the escalated incident.

Research further indicates that many incidents (and those which tend to be particularly violent) are related to excessive alcohol consumption, as well as to nicotine withdrawal symptoms of smokers. The service on board provided by the crew must take a responsible approach with regard to the serving of alcohol and should provide alternatives (such as nicotine gum) for smokers.

Measures to maximize prevention of incidents

Internally within the carrier by:

- providing staff with a clear written policy on how to deal with disruptive behaviour, especially in its early stages;
- ensuring a smooth operation: defusing the frustration that occurs over long waiting times, the flight being overbooked, lack of information, technical deficiencies, etc.;
- providing training for frontline staff. This includes instructing both ground staff and crew (flight deck and cabin) to learn how to recognize the early signs of potentially disruptive behaviour (e.g. drinking heavily); ensuring that those who come in contact with customers have acquired the necessary verbal skills and that they understand the importance of informing other operational areas of the situation to enable them to deal with the passenger effectively (not simply "passing" the passenger onwards without identifying that the passenger is showing early warning signs of potentially problematic behaviour);
- maintaining accurate and updated reports and statistics of incidents that do occur so as to continually monitor the types of incidents and identify potential training needs, etc.

Externally by communicating with passengers:

- prior to boarding, especially when groups are travelling together;
- by having dedicated information cards placed in seat pockets;
- through information on the flight ticket/e-receipt.

Source: adapted from IATA guide, 1998, op. cit., pp. 9–10.

> ## Box 4.5   Home visiting: Community nursing
>
> There is little doubt that community nurses have to deal with many difficult and abusive situations. From the limited data that exist, it would appear that incidents of violence tend to occur while nurses are making their way to or from the home. Incidents which do occur inside the home most often involve threats, verbal abuse and other anti-social behaviour, as opposed to physical violence.
>
> ### Search for preventive measures
>
> *The assailant:* In general, there is little that can be done to change the potential assailants. The policy to move previously institutionalized patients back into the community is resulting in more patients with a potential for violence. Where the potential assailants are people who might assault a nurse en route to a visit, there is probably little that can be done by the employer to intervene.
>
> *The employee.* Because of the mobile nature of community nursing, it is with the employee that measures can most easily be introduced. Some measures that have been suggested include:
>
> - Selection: The selection of experienced nurses with good social skills has been identified as important in maintaining low levels of violence.
> - Training: Improving the training and guidance available to community nurses has been requested by nurses. Training often focuses on what are likely to be difficult situations, what are the signs of potential violence and how to de-escalate aggression.
> - Training in self-defence: There are differing views as to whether this type of training is helpful or whether it has the effect of creating unnecessary fear and anxiety in nurses.
> - Not wearing uniforms: In some neighbourhoods, it is considered unhelpful to wear a uniform since it can be readily identified by would-be assailants who may be in search of drugs.
> - Radios and personal alarms: Although it has been said that these measures boost staff confidence, doubts have been expressed about the effect of this approach on the quality of the interaction with patients.
>
> *The interaction.* One option must always be to withdraw a service when a family member or individual becomes virtually impossible to deal with satisfactorily.
>
> *The work environment*
>
> - The timing of visits: If nurses have a choice when they visit their patients, it may be safer to make visits to dangerous areas during the earlier part of the day, and certainly during daylight.
> - Visiting in pairs: One approach to difficult visits is to arrange for nurses to visit in pairs.
> - Better information: It is important that nurses are fully briefed about their cases, especially if they are likely to be difficult.
>
> Source: adapted from B. Poyner and C. Warne: *Preventing violence to staff* (London, HSE, 1988), pp. 60–64. The information for this case study was derived from contact with a number of senior nursing staff involved in the management of community nursing services, based in the London area.

Nurses are another occupational group known to be at risk of Type 2 incidents, or incidents from patients/clients. A survey by the British National Health Service estimated that nearly 50 per cent of nurses had been physically attacked at work in the past year, while 85 per cent had been verbally abused.[22] Box 4.5 summarizes a case study that examines the field of community nursing and the preventive approaches being applied to the problem of workplace violence. Although this study focuses on community nurses, the preventive measures discussed are relevant for all workers who visit their clients at home (e.g. social workers, utility workers, etc.). Furthermore, the case study is an example of "best practice" in that it takes an integrative approach to prevention, considering the assailant, the employee and the working environment all as potential points of intervention.

In summary, preventing incidents perpetrated by customers or clients can be done using engineering (e.g. alarm systems), administrative (e.g. standard procedures for handling violent clients) and/or work practice controls (e.g. changes to service delivery). The practical examples discussed in this section, and the literature in this area, do not emphasize one form of control over the others. In fact, most sources suggest that the best solution is often a mix of different controls, or measures.

Addressing Type 3 risk factors

Background: Type 3 scenarios involve agents who are in some form of employment relationship (past or present) with the affected workplace, e.g. co-workers, supervisors. The Type 3 events identified by the original researchers in California were said to be more closely tied to employer–employee relations than the preceding events. As a result, the approach to prevention will be different from those for the other two types of violence:

> Employers who have employees with a history of assaults or who have exhibited belligerent, intimidating or threatening behavior in the workplace need to establish and implement procedures to respond to workplace security hazards when they are present and to provide training as necessary to their employees, supervisors and managers in order to satisfy the regulatory requirement of establishing, implementing and maintaining an effective IIP [Injury and Illness Prevention] Programme.

> Since Type 3 events are more closely tied to employer–employee relations than are Type 1 or 2 events, an employer's considerate and respectful management of his or her employees represents an effective strategy for preventing Type 3 events. Some workplace violence researchers have pointed out that employer actions which are perceived by an employee to place his or her continuing employment status in jeopardy can be triggering events for a workplace violence event, e.g. layoffs or reduction-in-force actions and disciplinary actions such as suspensions and terminations.

---

[22] Gallagher, op. cit., pp. 10–11.

Some mental health professionals believe that belligerent, intimidating and threatening behavior by an employee or supervisor is an early warning sign of an individual's propensity to commit a physical assault in the future, and that monitoring and responding to such behaviour is a necessary part of effective prevention.

Many management consultants who advise employers about workplace violence stress that to effectively prevent Type 3 events from occurring, employers need to establish a clear anti-violence management policy, apply the policy consistently and fairly to all employees, including supervisors and managers, and provide appropriate supervisory and employee training in workplace violence prevention.[23]

Practical examples: An issue of particular concern in addressing what can be broadly labelled as Type 3 risk factors is the development and articulation of general prevention strategies to deal with violence from insiders. Preventive measures for this type of violence include those which relate to "the dysfunctional organizational dynamics which produce or enable threatening behaviour by one employee to another to flourish".[24] Hence it is suggested that the best way to tackle this type of workplace violence is through the implementation of effective policies, procedures, training and organizational development efforts, as opposed to engineering controls. Ultimately, the best way to prevent this form of workplace violence is to develop a corporate culture that encourages and promotes respect, equality and open communication.[25] Here are some ways to build such a culture:[26]

- **Implement a workplace violence policy:** Organizations must communicate to employees that violence will not be tolerated. Through a policy they can define inappropriate behaviour and communicate what appropriate behaviour looks like. This will help to establish norms for respectful behaviour. Policies of this nature are described in greater detail later in the chapter.
- **Provide an environment that is physically comfortable:** Stress levels and the likelihood of violence increase with physical discomfort. Ensuring comfortable temperatures, high air quality, adequate lighting and manageable noise levels will all help to create a comfortable working environment conducive to work and associated with lower levels of stress.
- **Provide support for employees under stress:** Employers can offer assistance and support to their employees through programmes such as Employee Assistance Programmes (EAPs). These aim to help employees with their problems before they escalate into destructive behaviour. They can help with issues related to substance abuse, work-related stress, anxiety or depression, and many more.

---

[23] OSHA late-night retail guide, op. cit., pp. 11–15.

[24] Standing and Nicolini, op. cit., p. 49.

[25] C.E. Labig (RHR International Co.): *Preventing violence in the workplace* (New York, American Management Association, 1995), p. 141.

[26] Adapted from J.H. Neuman and R.A. Baron: "Workplace violence and workplace aggression: Evidence concerning specific forms, potential causes, and preferred targets", in *Journal of Management*, Vol. 24, No. 3, 1998, pp. 406–410.

- **Conduct training:** Training can provide employees with the skills necessary to manage their own anger and stress, and the skills to help them defuse anger in others. With regard to the former, this training can take the form of basic social skills to reduce the likelihood of violence. With regard to the latter (defusing others' anger), training in how to manage conflict, communicate effectively and deal with confrontational employees is helpful. More specific skills, such as how to deliver constructive feedback during a performance review, and how to effectively terminate an employee, may also prove useful.

Many of the influential guides provide valuable assistance to those wishing to produce comprehensive policies and procedures to deal with Type 3 violence. For example, reference is made in the Western Australian code of practice to a number of strategies that can be applied to general work arrangements to alleviate the threat of violence by internal employees. These include providing job rotation for workers exposed to highly stressful work situations; ensuring that new workers are not required to work alone until they achieve adequate competencies; and developing effective communication systems between workers to alert them to potentially violent situations.[27]

The American Federation of State, County and Municipal Employees (AFSCME) guide also contains helpful advice on addressing violence from internal employees within a unionized environment (box 4.6).

Harassment and bullying: The Australian Public Service Commission suggests that there are three main elements to any strategy for preventing workplace harassment. These include:[28]

1 Developing a written harassment policy statement on management's commitment to positive working relationships and practices in the workplace, including refusal to tolerate any form of workplace harassment. (Any harassment policy needs to take into account national and/or regional legislation related to this topic.)

2. Putting in place effective procedures to deal with incidents of alleged workplace harassment.

3. Providing information and training on the workplace harassment policy and procedures.

Although it is agreed that the development of an explicit and visible company policy is important to any thorough response to workplace harassment and bullying, there is still considerable variation in practice among policy-makers regarding appropriate ways of responding to this type of

---

[27] Western Australian code of practice, op. cit., pp. 14–20.

[28] Australian Public Service Commission: *Eliminating workplace harassment guidelines* (Canberra, Australian Government Publishing Service, 1994). This comprehensive guide, based upon the experience gained in implementing programmes to eradicate sexual harassment, canvasses issues and responses which can be applied well beyond the Australian public service.

Box 4.6   Violence among co-workers and managers

Violence among co-workers and managers can take many forms. For example, an individual worker may threaten other workers or his or her supervisor, a manager may harass workers, or a group of workers may act disrespectfully to their supervisors and each other, or behave in other inappropriate, potentially violent ways. To further complicate matters, the causes of this type of violence can be numerous, difficult to identify, and not always easy to resolve.

Some of the same factors associated with violence committed by patients, clients or intruders may also contribute to violence among co-workers and managers. Such factors include a lack of security, workplace layouts that trap employees behind furniture, inadequate escape routes and a lack of training.

But for conflicts occurring among employees or their managers, other factors may play a role. These may be caused by the workplace itself or stem from outside the workplace, such as personal problems that employees bring to work. Both workplace and non-workplace factors ought to be considered as potential causes of violent behaviour.

Workplace risk factors

Violence among workers and managers may be linked to the work climate and job stress. Signs of a troubled or at-risk work environment that could lead to worker-on-worker violence include:

- chronic labour–management disputes;
- frequent grievances filed by employees (or a marked reduction in the number of grievances if employees don't believe the system works);
- an extraordinary number of workers' compensation claims (especially for psychological illness or mental stress);
- understaffing or excessive demands for overtime;
- a high number of "stressed-out" workers;
- limited flexibility in how workers perform their jobs;
- pending or rumoured layoffs or "downsizing";
- significant changes in job responsibilities or workload;
- an authoritarian management style.

If the workplace creates the potential for violence, the union should urge management to correct the problems identified. By addressing problems in the work environment, the union and management may prevent employees from becoming threatening or violent.

Source: adapted from AFSCME guide, 1998, op. cit., Ch. 5.

**Box 4.7 Workplace violence prevention programme:
Sample policy statement**

[Effective date for programme]

Our establishment [employer name] is concerned and committed to our
employees' safety and health. We refuse to tolerate violence in the workplace
and will make every effort to prevent violent incidents from occurring by
implementing a Workplace Violence Prevention Programme (WPVP). We will
provide adequate authority and budgetary resources to responsible parties so
that our goals and responsibilities can be met.

All managers and supervisors are responsible for implementing and maintaining
our WPVP. We encourage employee participation in designing and
implementing our programme. We require prompt and accurate reporting of all
violent incidents whether or not physical injury has occurred. We will not
discriminate against victims of workplace violence.

A copy of this policy statement and our WPVP is readily available to all
employees from each manager and supervisor.

Our programme ensures that all employees, including supervisors and
managers, adhere to work practices that are designed to make the workplace
more secure, and do not engage in verbal threats or physical actions which
create a security hazard for others in the workplace.

All employees, including managers and supervisors, are responsible for using
safe work practices, for following all directives, policies and procedures, and for
assisting in maintaining a safe and secure work environment.

The management of our establishment is responsible for ensuring that all safety
and health policies and procedures involving workplace security are clearly
communicated and understood by all employees. Managers and supervisors
are expected to enforce the rules fairly and uniformly.

Our programme will be reviewed and updated annually.

Source: adapted from United States Department of Labor, Occupational Safety and Health
Administration (OSHA) and the Long Island Coalition for Workplace Violence Awareness and
Prevention: *Workplace violence awareness and prevention: An information and instructional
package for use by employers and employees* (Washington, DC, 1996), Part III
(Web site http://www.osha-slc.gov/workplace_violence/wrkplaceViolence.intro.html).

---

workplace violence.[29] The British survey of bullying at work, for example,
found that while almost two-thirds of all the organizations surveyed had some
kind of written policy, statement or guideline on bullying, these most

---

[29] H. Cowie et al.: "Measuring workplace bullying", in *Aggression and Violent Behavior*, Vol. 7, 2002, pp. 33–51; P.M.
Gleninning: "Workplace bullying: Curing the cancer of the American workplace", in *Public Personnel Management*, Vol.
30, No. 3, 2001, pp. 269–286; H. Leymann: "Mobbing and psychological terror in workplaces", in *Violence and Victims*,
Vol. 5, No. 2, 1990, pp. 119–126; C. Rayner, H. Hoel and C. L. Cooper: *Workplace bullying: What we know, who is to blame,
and what can we do?* (London, Taylor & Francis, 2002).

frequently took the form of a broader harassment policy into which bullying had been placed as one form of this behaviour.[30] The harassment policies that were in place varied in the degree to which they incorporated bullying from a single sentence mentioning this as one of many types of harassment, to jointly labelling the policy as one concerning "harassment and bullying", or "dignity at work".[31] Most of the organizations that had amended their harassment policies during the past two years had done so with the aim of giving more weight to bullying as a form of harassment alongside sexual and racial harassment.[32]

While a certain level of disagreement is likely to continue concerning the boundaries between harassment, bullying and workplace violence policies, there seems to be a growing consensus that each of these forms of behaviour is unacceptable and not to be tolerated at work (a sample workplace violence policy is provided in box 4.7). Thus, a recent proposal for a model policy on both harassment and bullying has suggested that it should:

- apply to all employees;
- contain a clear commitment from the very top of the organization to tackle harassment and bullying;
- be negotiated by management and trade unions;
- recognize that harassment and bullying are serious offences;
- recognize that bullying and harassment are issues for the whole organization;
- guarantee confidentiality;
- guarantee that complainants will not be victimized;
- include a statement that harassment and bullying are unacceptable and will not be tolerated at any level;
- include a statement that harassment and bullying will be treated as disciplinary offences;
- be stringently implemented; and
- include provision for the monitoring and review of the policy.[33]

Unlike the other two types of violence (i.e. those involving criminal intruders and clients/customers), the use of engineering controls is infrequently mentioned in the prevention of Type 3 incidents. Instead, there is a clear emphasis on administrative controls (e.g. establishing a clear anti-violence policy internally) and work practice controls (e.g. providing job rotation to workers in stressful roles).

---

[30] Industrial Relations Service (IRS): "Bullying at work: A survey of 157 employers", in *Employee Health Bulletin*, Vol. 8, Apr. 1999, p. 8.

[31] ibid.

[32] ibid.

[33] ibid, p. 8.

Education and training

Another vital component of any workplace violence prevention programme is the provision of education and training for all persons affected by its provisions (e.g. training on new policies, new reporting procedures, new systems, etc.). Each of the influential guidelines that has been referred to in this book emphasizes the need for training. Thus the CCOHS guide makes an explicit policy statement on providing workplace violence training and education (box 4.8).

As is pointed out in this excerpt, training and education must ensure that all staff are aware of the potential hazards in their working environment and how to protect themselves through established policies and procedures. Beyond general training for all employees, the CCOHS guide also highlights the importance of specialized training for those workers in jobs or locations that put them at a higher risk of workplace violence (this may involve training to provide employees with the skills necessary to reduce the risk of violence, such as conflict-resolution skills). Other guidelines go further to suggest that managers and supervisors should undergo additional training to cover topics such as:[34]

* how to recognize potentially hazardous situations;
* how to implement methods and procedures that will reduce or eliminate hazards in the working environment;
* how to ensure that employees follow safe work practices;
* how to behave towards employees when an incident does occur.

Clearly each organization or enterprise must determine its own education and training needs. Cost and related resource considerations may influence decisions about the nature and scope of the education and training that can be provided within a given workplace. Regardless of resource limitations, however, all enterprises have a responsibility to ensure that any violence prevention procedures are understood and followed, and that their staff are adequately prepared to respond to workplace violence, including being well briefed on how critical incidents will be dealt with should they occur (critical incident preparation is covered in Chapter 5).

Some important words of caution

Omissions and flaws

After describing the positive assistance and advice that can be obtained from these various approaches and influential guidelines regarding workplace violence prevention strategies, it is wise to add a caution about certain pitfalls that should be avoided in developing policy and procedures on this subject. As the AFSCME guide stresses, many workplace violence programmes initiated

---

[34] OSHA guide, op. cit., pp. 6–7; OPM guide, op. cit., pp. 20–21.

Box 4.8   Providing workplace violence training and education

Education and training are an indispensable part of any violence prevention programme. The exact content and type of training necessary depend upon the results of your workplace risk assessment and your workplace-specific prevention programme.

All employees need to understand:

- their rights and responsibilities under any relevant legislation and company policy;
- the scope of workplace violence and risk factors;
- your organization's prevention policy;
- your organization's procedures and arrangements to minimize or control the risk of violence;
- safe and appropriate responses to incidents or potential incidents, including how to obtain assistance;
- the correct procedures for reporting, investigating and documenting incidents or potential incidents;
- the follow-up and support services that are available to them, in the event of a violent incident.

Training should be specific to the risk of each individual employee or occupational category and may cover the following:

- warning signs that may precede a violent situation;
- how to prepare a profile of a potentially violent client;
- ways of preventing or defusing volatile situations or aggressive behaviour, including:
  - anger management;
  - mediation;
  - interpersonal skills;
  - conflict resolution;
  - behaviour management;
  - assertiveness training;
- stress management, relaxation techniques and wellness training;
- crisis intervention.

Effective training will use techniques such as role playing, simulations and drills. Periodic refresher courses are necessary.

Source: adapted from CCOHS guide, 1999, op. cit., pp. 28–29.

by employers are produced in the belief that most violence is caused by disgruntled employees.[35] Organizations should not fall into the trap of designing policies to deal with high-profile disgruntled employee physical attacks which are in fact few in number. They must recognize the variety of sources from which aggression comes and make sure that it is reflected in comprehensive policies.

The AFSCME guide goes on to identify and describe some of the common characteristics of flawed policies and programmes. The flawed programmes generally result, according to the AFSCME guide, from an attempt to deal only with a single category of violence – that involving workers and managers. Some of the common flaws and omissions are described further in box 4.9.

Other common mistakes made by organizations in their attempt to prevent violence at work include:[36]

- believing that their organization is immune from violence;
- failing to document incidents in an adequate manner;
- not taking threats seriously;
- failing to articulate a strong policy against violence;
- not enforcing the violence prevention policy or following disciplinary procedures;
- relying overly on physical security measures (e.g. alarms and cameras); and
- not providing appropriate support to victims of violence.

Unintended side effects

It is important to understand that while prevention strategies may reduce the risk of violence, they may also produce negative or unintended results.[37] Possible unintended side effects may include:

- implementing engineering controls, or protective barriers, that are perceived as aggressive by clients or that interfere with the provision of required services;
- implementing security or surveillance devices that are perceived as an intrusion on employees' privacy; and
- raising the awareness of staff regarding the issue of workplace violence, and having this increased awareness degenerate into fear.

Most of the measures suggested for preventing violence do bear some risks. Organizations must use common sense to balance security needs with factors such as cost and privacy.

---

[35] AFSCME guide, op. cit., Ch. 8.

[36] CCOHS guide, op. cit., p. 126; J.A. Kinney: *Violence at work: How to make your company safe for employees and customers* (Englewood Cliffs, NJ, Prentice Hall, 1995), pp. 177–185.

[37] Standing and Nicolini, op. cit., p. 57.

Box 4.9 Common programme flaws and omissions

Profiles

Employers often attempt to match workers to certain violent traits on a list of "profiles" in order to predict who will become violent in the future. Management consultants often use these profiles to make money by allegedly helping employers to "recognize" potentially violent employees before they are hired, identify any current employees who may become violent, and discipline, fire and "downsize" employees without violence. Most professionals have serious problems with profiling. These problems include the following:

- Sometimes these profiles may be useful in the hands of trained professionals, but managers and untrained persons can use them to label and harass workers.
- After a violent incident occurs, it is easy to fit the assailant into a profile, but most people who fit many items on a profile will never become violent.
- Almost anyone can become violent if pushed beyond a certain point.
- Profiles sometimes use race, sex or age criteria that may violate anti-discrimination laws.
- Profiles can make things worse if an employee who may indeed become violent is singled out in a negative way.
- Even where profiling has some value in predicting future behaviour, the time ahead that such behaviour can be predicted is usually too short to be of real use.

Employers should take responsibility for employees who exhibit truly threatening behaviour that has a potential for violence, not just because they fit a certain profile.

Psychological tests

Like profiling, psychological testing of workers for violent tendencies attempts to predict which employees will commit future violence. Often done as part of the pre-employment process, psychological testing policies that try to separate the safe workers from the potentially violent ones may be impractical and illegal. Although employers may have a legal responsibility to avoid negligent hiring, administering psychological tests may raise confidentiality issues, as well as infringe rights that workers have under such laws as the Americans with Disabilities Act. Furthermore, psychological tests may not be effective or reliable. Experience with psychological tests has shown that most perpetrators commit violence at a time beyond the predictive scope of the tests.

"Zero-tolerance" policies

Zero-tolerance policies – policies that prohibit certain behaviour or comments – are often the only response by some employers to workplace violence hazards. Although it is important for managers and workers to have clear guidelines for unacceptable behaviour – especially unacceptable behaviour such as actual physical assaults by employees on management or other employees – there are several problems with zero-tolerance policies.

continued

First, some employers believe that just issuing a piece of paper that prohibits employees from doing or saying "violent" things will prevent workplace violence, regardless of what other working conditions may be contributing to a violent atmosphere. In addition, a zero-tolerance policy may ignore the contract and violate the principle of progressive discipline. Finally, a zero-tolerance policy may go too far in defining threatening language or behaviour.

Zero-tolerance policies may be abused by management. For instance, a supervisor may find it easy to intentionally provoke an employee into losing his or her temper. The employee may never be given a chance to defend or explain his or her comments or behaviour. Under some zero-tolerance policies, making an offhand, not serious, comment or innocent joke, no matter what the circumstances, may be grounds for immediate dismissal.

Some zero-tolerance policies define "threatening language" as a cause for automatic dismissal. Because of the cultural diversity in American society, however, people of varying ethnic, racial, religious, generational or economic groups may use different language and gestures to express themselves. Natural and harmless expressions by one group may be perceived by another as aggressive and threatening. For example, a person's voice may become louder and her gestures more animated when she gets excited, not necessarily because she is angry or hostile. While any kind of hostile or threatening language is not acceptable in the workplace, some language may be misinterpreted.

When negotiating any kind of zero-tolerance policy with management, it is important to review the contract to determine if any workplace violence prevention policy violates any of the contract provisions or can be used by management to harass employees.

Threat-assessment teams

Threat-assessment teams, also called crisis intervention teams, are sometimes created by management to enforce zero-tolerance policies. Generally, the purpose of these teams is to receive, investigate and respond to reports of threats to determine the potential for violence. Some teams even go so far as to try to defuse a potentially violent situation.

Teams that try only to identify potentially violent situations and recommend procedures for responding to those situations may be effective in curbing internal problems of violence, as long as they do not take actions that might endanger themselves or anyone else. For a team to be effective, it should have an equal number of trained managers and union representatives. Such teams should also include mental health professionals. Without proper training and years of experience in a mental health discipline, lay people are likely to reach wrong conclusions and may put themselves and others at risk in dangerous situations.

continued

Policies that exclude the union

Workplace violence programmes or threat-assessment teams that do not have union-designated representatives will have little credibility with employees, will tend to blame non-managerial workers for problems and will inevitably fail to effectively address the problem of workplace violence.

One-sided management policies

Policies that are not applied equally to both managerial and non-managerial employees may lead to further labour–management conflict. All violence prevention strategies, particularly zero-tolerance policies, should be applied equally to all levels of employees since managers and supervisors can also cause physical violence, threats and harassment. Since workers may have violence-related problems with their supervisors, these policies may have little credibility with employees.

Source: adapted from AFSCME guide, 1998, op. cit., Ch. 8.

STEP 3 – DESIGN AND IMPLEMENT REACTIVE MEASURES

5

The risk-management process

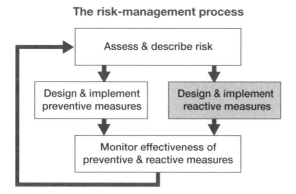

Why design and implement reactive measures?

The clear goal of any workplace violence prevention strategy is to eliminate or minimize the probability of an incident of violence taking place. Unfortunately, despite the best policies and procedures put in place to secure a workplace against the threat of violence, incidents can still occur. It is for this reason that a systematic approach to the issue of workplace violence should also include the design and implementation of reactive measures to address incidents as they arise and to help in preventing future incidents.

Two basic questions need to be answered through this third step in the risk-management process:

1. *How do we make sure that we are prepared to respond quickly and effectively in the case of a critical incident or an emergency situation (e.g. an armed robbery, a physical attack, a threat to someone's life)?* It is often recommended that workplace violence prevention plans contain policies and procedures which assist with the immediate response after an incident, the process of recovery and the review of the circumstances involved.

deployed as required.[3] The composition of such a team should be diverse, with representatives from departments such as human resources, security, legal, medical services and public relations, as well as external professional care providers. The individuals in a crisis response team should be responsible for developing and communicating procedures to be adhered to in the event of a violent episode, as well as the activities already described.

Some of the guidelines in this area provide response suggestions for a range of violent situations. For example, the CCOHS guide sets out a range of practical suggestions on how to respond to incidents involving physical attack, hostage situations, robbery and bomb threats. This guide also provides suggestions about measures that can be taken to defuse the potential for violence when dealing with aggressive individuals or risky situations in the workplace.[4] Since the CCOHS guide is concerned principally with enterprises that are governed by the framework of occupational health and safety legislation in Canada and the United States, the advice it contains must be tempered by the knowledge that the parameters of the North American legislative and regulatory regimes on this subject do not necessarily equate with those found in Europe and other regions of the world.

Immediate response and recovery

After securing the work area and ensuring the physical safety of employees, an organization's focus must turn to the physical and emotional well-being of those staff directly and indirectly involved in the incident. Guidance on the recovery phase of a workplace violence prevention strategy can be obtained from a number of influential guideline sources. As the Western Australian code of practice states:

> The recovery phase is about employees returning to normal duties as quickly as possible after the disruptive incident. In this phase, plans previously agreed should be implemented as quickly and efficiently as possible to reduce the risk of long term problems. The following actions should be part of the process:
>
> * provide clear information to all employees;
>
> * provide ongoing professional counselling and support services for employees and their families;
>
> * allow employees time to recover but encourage early return to work as part of the recovery process;
>
> * provide advice on legal matters and workers' compensation arrangements as appropriate; and
>
> * investigate the incident and review safety management to reduce the risk of injury or harm in the future.[5]

---

[3] Perrone, op. cit., p. 86; OSHA guide, op. cit., p. 8.

[4] See in general CCOHS guide, op. cit., Section IV, pp. 102–124.

[5] Western Australian code of practice, op. cit., p. 22.

Box 5.2   Reacting to violence after it occurs

Apart from physical injuries, violent or threatening incidents in the workplace often result in serious and disabling psychological damage. While bruises, wounds or broken bones may heal in days or months, the emotional trauma of a violent attack may take years to subside. After implementing the emergency action plan and providing prompt medical treatment for victims of workplace violence, employers will also have to deal with the psychological effects of violence.

Even supervisors who are sensitive to emotional trauma may not recognize that a violent incident – even one that does not result in a physical injury – can have serious and long-lasting psychological effects on an employee.

Immediately after an incident, critical incident debriefing should occur with all affected staff. Victims of the assault, as well as their co-workers, need the opportunity to discuss their concerns and feelings about the incident, and suggest how to prevent such incidents from happening again.

Victims of workplace violence have an increased risk of long-term emotional problems and post-traumatic stress disorder (PTSD), which is common among combat veterans and victims of terrorism, crime, rape and other violent incidents. Symptoms include self-doubt, depression, fear, sleep disturbances, irritability, reduced ability to function at work, increased absenteeism, and disturbed relationships with family, friends and co-workers. Workers often blame themselves when they are injured in an assault, and management may encourage this self-blame. Victims and witnesses of violence often need long-term treatment to overcome these problems.

Fear of reprisal and lack of support for workers who are victims of violence discourage workers from reporting incidents and may lead to needless trauma for victims, co-workers and witnesses.

Employers, in cooperation with the union, should establish a process where post-trauma counselling is provided to all staff and their families who want it. The counselling should be done by a well-trained professional who understands the issues of assault and its consequences. Workers who witness incidents and co-workers who do the same jobs as the assault victim (even if at a different location) may also need assistance.

Source: adapted from AFSCME guide, 1998, op. cit., Ch. 7.

Experiencing a violent event at work can be extremely traumatic for those employees involved and, if not dealt with appropriately, can have both short-term and long-term effects on their health. The AFSCME guide describes the negative consequences that are often associated with traumatic events and those steps that employers can take to help prevent their occurrence (box 5.2).

The OPM guide also offers advice on how managers can help affected employees recover after an incident of workplace violence (box 5.3). Although

Box 5.3   Recovery steps

Ensure a management presence in the worksite
Managers need to spend ample time with their employees, in the worksite or wherever they may be. Employees need to be reassured of their concern, and they need to be able to ask questions. Senior management needs to serve as a "buffer zone" to ensure that immediate supervisors are supported in this role, relieved of unnecessary duties, and not pulled away from their subordinates to write lengthy reports or prepare elaborate briefings.

Share information with employees
Employees will have many questions, and they need the answers – often more than once – if they are to resolve the experience for themselves. Information will develop over time, so information strategies need to be simple and fluid. A notice-board at the elevator, or a recorded message on a "hotline" number, may suffice for the basics, and a user-friendly system for individual questions needs to be established.

Include union leadership
Union representatives can help in reassuring employees after an incident and in getting information to employees.

Bring in crisis response professionals
Before an incident ever occurs, the planning group should identify trained mental health professionals in the agency's Employee Assistance Programme or the community who would be available to respond in the event of an incident. When an incident occurs, involve these emergency mental health consultants as soon as possible. They will generally need to meet with management first, working down the chain, and then with line employees. Based on what the consultants learn, they will offer services such as debriefing and defusing the situation, and information counselling, perhaps in the work area.

Support informal debriefing
The formal debriefing doesn't end the recovery process. Provide opportunities for employees to talk informally with one another when they feel a need to discuss the experience. A comfortable break area and flexibility about break times may be all that is needed.

Support care-giving within work groups
Keep work groups together as much as possible, and try not to isolate employees from their normal support groups at work. Show respect and support for employees' efforts to care for one another.

Handle critical sites with care
Initially, the site of a violent incident will be secured as a crime scene. After the authorities have finished with it, management needs to be sensitive to a number of issues. It is helpful if employees don't have to come back to work and face

continued

painful reminders such as blood stains or broken furniture. But on the other hand, the area should not be so "sanitized" that it gives the appearance that management is pretending nothing happened. If someone has died, that person's work area will be a focus of grieving, and it needs to be respected as such.

Buffer those affected from post-event stresses
Effective coordination with the media and timely dissemination of information can help reduce media pressure on those who are the most vulnerable. Assistance with benefits and other administrative issues can reduce the burden on victims and families.

Help employees face feared places or activities
Remember the old saying about getting back on the horse. Returning soon, if only briefly, to a feared site can help prevent lasting effects such as phobic responses. Bringing a friend or loved one along, or being supported by close work associates, may make the first step much easier.

Remember the healing value of work
Getting back to work can be reassuring, and a sense of having a mission to perform can help the group recover its morale. But the return to work must be managed in a way that conveys appropriate respect for the deceased, the injured and the traumatized.

Source: adapted from OPM guide, 1998, op. cit., pp. 133–135.

these suggestions contain elements that are relevant to all organizations trying to cope with workplace violence, they are of principal relevance to larger enterprises in the public and private sectors.

The Western Australian code of practice, the AFSCME guide and the OPM guide each emphasizes the importance of involving professional counselling and support services in the recovery phase. For years mental health experts have used formal crisis intervention processes for victims of traumatic events, including incidents of workplace violence.[6] Among the processes recommended are debriefing sessions, which allow victims to talk through their experience with their co-workers and supervisor (debriefing is recommended in all but the most trivial cases), and professional trauma counselling. Crisis intervention processes of this nature are known to reduce the acute psychological trauma and general stress levels experienced by victims and witnesses.[7]

---

[6] The OPM guide provides a number of references to the professional literature in this field, as well as setting out basic crisis management principles. See OPM guide, op. cit., pp. 135–141.

[7] Chappell and Di Martino, op. cit., p. 122.

Investigation and review

Integral to the recovery and review process is the establishment of the factual circumstances surrounding an incident of workplace violence. By gaining an understanding of why and how an incident took place it may be possible to take remedial action to prevent a similar happening in the future. As with all other phases in the risk-management process, it is important that employees are consulted and their suggestions taken into consideration during this review process. Two case studies (boxes 5.4 and 5.5) can assist in illustrating how an understanding of an incident can help to identify measures that may prevent similar events from occurring in the future.[8]

Where an incident of violence is clearly one which amounts to a crime, as in the case studies just outlined, a formal investigation will almost certainly be launched immediately by a responsible law enforcement agency. The way in which this investigation is conducted lies outside the scope of this book. (It should be noted that the OPM guide provides advice regarding the types of investigation which can be conducted after an incident of violence, e.g. criminal versus administrative, and the use of workplace violence investigators.[9]) From a workplace perspective, the principal responsibility of those involved in an incident of this gravity is twofold: (1) to handle critical sites with care and sensitivity; and (2) to conduct an internal review, not for the purposes of fault-finding but for fact-finding and future prevention. An internal investigation of this sort should:[10]

- collect facts on who, what, when, where and how the incident occurred;
- record information;
- identify contributing causes;
- recommend corrective action;
- encourage appropriate follow-up; and
- consider changes in controls, procedures and policy.

If the incident of violence which has taken place, or is alleged to have taken place, does not appear to require an immediate criminal justice response, it is the workplace that will bear the primary responsibility for investigating and reviewing the surrounding circumstances. The framework within which this investigation and review are conducted should form part of a workplace violence prevention plan. In larger enterprises this framework is likely to involve a formal administrative process linked to the handling of other types of

---

[8] The Berkeley, OPM and AFSCME guides each contain a number of case studies like these which can be a very valuable aid to promoting discussion and debate about issues associated with workplace violence. As such, they can be used in training, and in the planning process for developing an effective workplace violence prevention strategy.

[9] OPM guide, op. cit., pp. 80–86.

[10] OSHA guide, op. cit., p. 8.

Box 5.4   Case study: Taxi driver robbed

A female cab driver in San Francisco picked up a male passenger. He acted extremely nervous, was dressed in a heavy overcoat on a hot day, and kept one hand stuffed in his pocket. He gave a street address that sounded suspicious, but said, "I'll tell you how to get there".

He directed her to a cul-de-sac, next to a vacant lot. When they arrived, he stuck a gun in her neck and robbed her. Then he told her to get into the back seat of the cab and threatened her with sexual assault. She managed to get out of the cab and run to a nearby house, where she called the police. The man was apprehended within the hour.

"From the beginning", the driver recalls, "I was suspicious of the man's behaviour. But I didn't know how to get him out of the cab".

Through the efforts of the cab drivers' union, San Francisco recently adopted the first cab driver protection law in the United States. It requires cab companies to provide safety training, automatic door locks and other equipment to protect drivers.

What might have helped?

• Better training for drivers on how to act in dangerous situations.

• Refusing to take passengers who act in a suspicious manner.

• A bullet-proof shield in the cab.

• "Hazard lights" on the cab to notify the police of a problem.

• An emergency button in the cab linked to a global positioning device, to allow the dispatcher to track the cab's location.

• An "immediate voice access" radio system to notify the dispatcher of trouble.

Source: adapted from Berkeley guide, 1997, op. cit., p. 37.

© Labor Occupational Health Program, University of California at Berkeley.

---

established or alleged misconduct within the workplace (e.g. process for investigating claims of sexual harassment).

The Australian State of New South Wales has produced a new and helpful guide to intervention strategies that can be instituted in smaller enterprises when incidents of workplace violence (including bullying and harassment) have been identified or suspected.[11] It is designed to meet the particular needs

---

[11] Workcover New South Wales and the National Children's and Youth Law Centre (NCYLC): *Workplace violence: Intervention strategies for your business. A secure workplace for young Australians* (Sydney, 2000, 2001); http://www.workcover.nsw.gov.au/html/bullying.asp.

Box 5.5   Case study: Social worker attacked

A social worker was attacked while investigating a reported case of child abuse. "I was removing some children from a very bad environment", he remembers. "I tried to enter the house, but they wouldn't let me in. So I followed procedure and called for police assistance."

Once inside the house, he saw how bad the situation really was. "I could see the children had to be removed for their own safety. There were human faeces on the floor, rotten food, soiled clothing, drug paraphernalia." The social worker and police officer were unaware that at least 12 people lived in the house. When they entered, only the mother and father appeared to be there.

"Suddenly, from out of nowhere, people started rushing in", the social worker recalls. "Several of them jumped the police officer, and he went down. I was unarmed, and was kicked in the groin. When I went down, they started stomping on my head."

Since the attack, the social worker has been diagnosed with post-traumatic stress disorder. He has trouble sleeping. He has nightmares and cold sweats. He's tense all the time. His union, citing the Americans with Disabilities Act, arranged for his transfer to a desk job.

What might have helped?

- Briefing the social worker in advance about the situation, with information from all relevant agencies.
- Providing more police back-up when advance information indicates a serious threat.
- Training the social worker in danger assessment and appropriate response.
- Personal alarm or cellular phone.

Source: adapted from Berkeley guide, 1997, op. cit., p. 39.

© Labor Occupational Health Program, University of California at Berkeley.

---

of young people, who are frequently the main victims of bullying or harassment within the workplace. The section of this guide that discusses how to proceed upon receiving a complaint of bullying or harassment, including the investigative process, is reproduced in box 5.6.[12]

---

[12] This guide also contains models for a grievance procedure, a protocol for commencing the investigation of a complaint of non-criminal bullying or harassment, a record of interview and a conduct of interview schedule.

Box 5.6   Workplace violence: Intervention strategies for your business

When you receive a complaint of bullying and harassment

- Don't panic. You have a complaint procedure. Follow it.
- Make sure the complainant knows how it works. Give him or her a copy of the procedure.
- Make sure the complaint is documented. You write down what the person says, or they put it in their own words. Check you have it right. Ask how the complainant wants the matter dealt with – as a disciplinary matter, or (if there is a "soft" option) through mediation or counselling.
- Make sure that the complainant has some support or counselling. This cannot come from you, if you are doing the investigation or are responsible for discipline, but it is your responsibility to make sure that they get it.
- Make sure that the proper person gets the complaint for investigation. It might be you. But avoid conflicts of interest. No one should investigate a bullying or harassment complaint if they are a personal friend of either party, unless they are authorized by the employer. No one should investigate a complaint if the complainant thinks that he or she is the complainant's friend. People cannot be "impartial" and help to resolve it through mediation if they have taken sides. And a manager who has responsibility for discipline can't be a "mediator".
- Take steps to protect the complainant. He or she must not be victimized for having complained. Complainants must not be moved, unless they ask for this, and then only temporarily until the complaint is dealt with, or if they otherwise ask to go back to their place of work. If necessary, the alleged bully or harasser may be moved (or suspended, but always on full pay).
- Confidentiality must always be maintained. The complainant, all witnesses and the respondent must be told that there is to be no gossip or ganging up and taking sides, and that it will be a serious breach of discipline if they disobey this instruction while the complaint is being investigated or mediated.

Investigation

Some key issues are:

Natural justice and due process: "Natural justice" means that people accused of wrong-doing that might result in disciplinary or other adverse action have the right to know what they are accused of, and by whom; the right to respond and give their side of the story; and the right of a decision to be made by someone who has not prejudged the issue.

This does not mean that during the investigation it is impossible to take steps to protect the complainant.

Someone accused of harassing another person can be suspended – on full pay – if this is necessary for the investigation to take place.

Barriers to communication: There are major problems in getting details of workplace violence or harassment and bullying, especially in a workplace where

continued

these are perpetrated by older men on younger and more vulnerable employees with lesser experience: the code of silence, the "don't inform on your workmates" culture; refusal of young men to complain because of a "macho" culture; embarrassment, anger, tears, frustration, shame that they did not cope; and the genuine fear, reasonably held, of victimization.

These are best addressed through a code of conduct; clear processes; a swift investigation; and a clear message from the senior managers that those who cooperate will not be penalized for doing so.

Documentation: The investigation process should be well documented.

* You must document any complaint and/or reasons for investigation.
* You must document who explained the procedure to affected staff, and how and when it was explained.
* You must take notes of any interviews. Keep the notes separately from any personnel file and in a secure way.
* When interviewing people formally, you should ask them to sign the interview protocol – which warns them about confidentiality and explains the process – and keep it. You should give them a copy of the protocol for their information.
* Keep all documentation in a confidential file.
* Always write down exactly what they say: do not put it in your own words. You will have to read it back to the person to make sure you have it right. Do not write down any opinion of your own. These notes might be called for later by a court or tribunal.

Source: adapted from Workcover New South Wales and the National Children's and Youth Law Centre, 2000, 2001, op. cit.

© WorkCover NSW.

Disciplinary rules and procedures

Disciplinary rules and procedures are an important part of the process by which an organization responds to workplace violence. In fact, the use of disciplinary rules and procedures that lack fairness and consistency can be a potential trigger for workplace violence. The quotation below illustrates three important points with respect to the administration of disciplinary rules and procedures: (1) always complete the investigation before administering any disciplinary procedures; (2) administer disciplinary procedures in a careful and consistent manner when they are deemed appropriate; and (3) ensure that the rights of the complainant and the alleged harasser are maintained at all times throughout the process.

Once the investigation is complete, and recommendations for action are made, it is essential that any disciplinary measures are carefully carried out in order to maintain the rights of the harasser. Linking investigations to disciplinary procedures is a difficult area. However, to make the link distinct, the investigation should be viewed as a preliminary exercise, the purpose of which is to decide whether or not there is a case for disciplinary action. There are some cases in which incidents of harassment are considered to be gross misconduct, and the penalties for harassers need to be carried through – this is the stage where employees will assess the organization's serious intent to stamp out discrimination. The conflicting messages between policy and practice can be damaging if an organization does not act appropriately at this point.[13]

Dismissal is the ultimate sanction which employers have against employee misconduct. However, other than in the most serious incidents of violence, employers should have a range of disciplinary options at their disposal (e.g. reprimands, warnings, suspensions, reductions in grade). Whatever form the disciplinary process takes, employers have an obligation to ensure that workers are treated according to the principles of natural justice and fairness.[14]

Case study examples

The last section of this chapter presents two case studies (boxes 5.7 and 5.8) derived from real-life situations in American Federal agencies. These case studies are taken from the OPM guide and are intended as learning tools for other employers who are in the process of developing workplace violence prevention programmes. Each case study is structured in a similar fashion, with a description of the incident, the response and the resolution of the incident, and concluding with questions to encourage reflection and discussion. The OPM guide provides the following added direction:

> As you read the case studies, keep in mind that there is no one correct way to handle each situation. The case studies should not be taken as specific models of how to handle certain types of situations. Rather, they should be a starting point for a discussion and exploration of how a team approach can be instituted and adapted to the specific needs and requirements of your agency.[15]

The two case studies chosen for inclusion here involve threatening or intimidating behaviour between co-workers (i.e. Type 3 incidents). These examples illustrate how some cases involving threatening behaviour can be handled effectively by a supervisor (with support from others), while other cases may require the help of a threat-assessment professional. Moreover, the cases demonstrate the importance of taking all reports of workplace violence seriously, and of responding to each report objectively.

---

[13] Ishmael with Alemoru, op. cit., p. 215.

[14] Incomes Data Services (IDS): *Disciplinary procedures*, IDS Study 640 (London, 1997). This study, conducted in the United Kingdom, provides valuable advice about "best practice" approaches to the disciplinary process. It involves an examination of 50 disciplinary procedures from organizations in a wide variety of industries. The study contains extracts from a range of company documents and includes four disciplinary procedures in their entirety – from Boots The Chemists (a national chain); Halifax (a large building society and banking enterprise); Railtrack (the national railtrack operator); and Severn Trent Water (a large water utility).

[15] OPM guide, op. cit., p. 30.

Box 5.7 Case study: Frightening behaviour

The incident

A supervisor contacts the Employee Relations Office because one of his employees is making the other employees in the office uncomfortable. He said the employee does not seem to have engaged in any actionable misconduct but, because of the agency's new workplace violence policy, and the workplace violence training he had just received, he thought he should at least mention what was going on. The employee was recently divorced and had been going through a difficult time for over two years, and had made it clear that he was having financial problems which were causing him to be stressed out. He was irritable and aggressive in his speech much of the time. He would routinely talk about the number of guns he owned, not in the same sentence, but in the same general conversation in which he would mention that someone else was causing all of his problems.

Response

At the first meeting with the supervisor, the employee relations specialist and Employee Assistance Programme (EAP) counsellor suggested that, since this was a long-running situation rather than an immediate crisis, the supervisor would have time to do some fact-finding. They gave him several suggestions on how to do this while safeguarding the privacy of the employee (for example, request a confidential conversation with previous supervisors, go back to co-workers who registered complaints for more information, and, if he was not already familiar with the employee's personnel records, consult his file to see if there were previous adverse actions in it). Two days later they had another meeting to discuss the case and come up with a plan of action.

The supervisor's initial fact-finding showed that the employee's co-workers attributed his aggressive behaviour to the difficult divorce situation he had been going through, but they were nevertheless afraid of him. The supervisor did not learn any more specifics about why they were afraid, except that he was short-tempered, ill-mannered and spoke a lot about his guns (although, according to the co-workers, in a matter-of-fact rather than in an intimidating manner).

After getting ideas from the employee relations specialist and the EAP counsellor, the supervisor sat down with the employee and discussed his behaviour. He told the employee it was making everyone uncomfortable and that it must stop. He referred the employee to the EAP, setting a time and date.

Resolution

As a result of counselling by the supervisor and by the EAP counsellor, the employee changed his behaviour. He was unaware that his behaviour was scaring people. He learned new ways from the EAP to deal with people. He accepted the EAP referral to a therapist in the community to address underlying personal problems. Continued monitoring by the supervisor showed the employee's conduct improving to an acceptable level and remaining that way.

continued

Questions

1. Do you agree with the agency's approach in this case?

2. Can you think of other situations that would lend themselves to this kind of low-key approach?

3. Does your agency have effective EAP training so that supervisors are comfortable in turning to the EAP for advice?

Source: adapted from OPM guide, 1998, op. cit., pp. 68–69.

Box 5.8   Case study: Intimidation

The incident

An employee called a member of the agency crisis team for advice, saying that a co-worker was picking on her, and expressing fear that something serious might happen. For several weeks, she said, a co-worker had been making statements like: "You actually took credit for my work and you're spreading rumours that I'm no good. If you ever get credit for my work again, that will be the last time you take credit for anybody's work. I'll make sure of that." She also said that her computer files had been altered on several occasions and she suspected that it was the same co-worker. When she reported the situation to her supervisor, he tried to convince her that there was no real danger and that she was blowing things out of proportion. However, she continued to worry. She said she spoke with her union representative, who suggested she contact the agency's workplace violence team.

Response

The agency's plan called for the initial involvement of Employee Relations and the Employee Assistance Programme (EAP) in situations involving intimidation. The employee relations specialist and the EAP counsellor met with the supervisor. He told them he was aware of the situation, but that the woman who reported it tended to exaggerate. He knew the alleged perpetrator well, had supervised him for years, and said: "He just talks that way; he's not really dangerous." He gave examples of how the alleged perpetrator was all talk and not likely to act out. One example had occurred several months earlier when he had talked to the alleged perpetrator about his poor performance. The employee had become agitated and accused the supervisor of being unfair, siding with the other employees, and believing the rumours the co-workers were spreading about him. He stood up and in an angry voice said: "You'd better start treating me fairly or you're going to be the one with the problem." He then stormed out of the room, saying: "Don't ever forget my words." The supervisor reasoned that, since he had always been this way, he was not a real threat to anyone.

continued

During the initial meeting, the team encouraged the supervisor to take disciplinary action, but he didn't believe it was appropriate. They asked him to at least sign a written statement about these incidents. He was reluctant to make any kind of written statement and could not be persuaded by their arguments to do so.

The employee relations specialist conducted an investigation. The results confirmed continuing intimidating behaviour on the part of the alleged perpetrator. In interviews with the co-workers of the victim, they confirmed the menacing behaviour of the perpetrator and several felt threatened themselves. None was willing to sign affidavits. The investigator also found a witness to the incident where the supervisor had been threatened. As the alleged perpetrator had left the supervisor's office and passed by the secretary's desk, he had said: "He's an [expletive] and he'd better watch himself." Although he did not directly threaten the secretary, she also was intimidated by the perpetrator and said he often acted in a menacing fashion. However, the secretary was also unwilling to sign an affidavit.

After confirming the validity of the allegations, but with the supervisor refusing to take action, and the only affidavit being from the employee who originally reported the situation, the team considered three courses of action:

1. arrange for the reassignment of the victim to a work situation that eliminated the current threatening situation;
2. report the situation to the second-line supervisor and recommend that she propose disciplinary action against the perpetrator; and
3. locate an investigator with experience in workplace violence cases to conduct interviews with the reluctant witnesses. The investigator would be given a letter of authorization from the director of the office stating the requirement that employees must cooperate in the investigation or face disciplinary action.

The team located an investigator who was experienced in workplace violence cases from a nearby federal agency and worked out an inter-agency agreement to obtain his services. During the investigation, he showed the letter of authorization to only one employee and to the supervisor, since he was able to persuade the others to sign written affidavits without resorting to showing them the letter.

The agency security specialist met with the perpetrator to inform him that he was to have no further contact with the victim. He also met with the victim to give her advice on how to handle a situation like this if it were to happen again. In addition, he recommended a procedure to the team that would monitor computer use in the division. This action resulted in evidence showing that the employee was, in fact, altering computer files.

Resolution

The first-line supervisor was given a written reprimand by the second-line supervisor for failing to take proper action in a timely manner and for failing to ensure a safe work environment. He was counselled about the poor performance

continued

of his supervisory duties. The alleged perpetrator was charged with both disruptive behaviour and gaining malicious access to a non-authorized computer. Based on this information, he was removed from Federal Services.

Questions

1. Would supervisory training probably have resulted in quicker action against the perpetrator?

2. Do you have other approaches for persuading a recalcitrant supervisor to take action?

3. Do you have other approaches for persuading reluctant witnesses to give written statements?

4. Are you aware of the problems associated with requiring the subject of an investigation to give statements?

5. If you had not been able to persuade the reluctant witnesses to give written statements, and you only had the one affidavit to support the one incident, do you think this would have provided your agency with enough evidence to take disciplinary action? If so, what type of penalty would probably be given in this case?

Source: adapted from OPM guide, 1998, op. cit., pp. 65–67.

STEP 4 – MONITOR THE EFFECTIVENESS OF PREVENTIVE AND REACTIVE MEASURES

6

The risk-management process

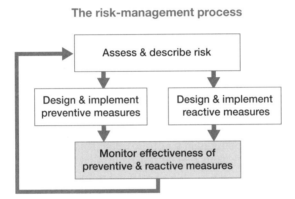

The purpose of evaluation

Monitoring the effectiveness of preventive and reactive measures is the fourth and final step in the risk-management process. Although often overlooked, this step is extremely important since it is through the evaluation process that an organization determines whether the actions taken to eliminate hazards and reduce risk have been successful. Further, the information gathered through the evaluation process serves as key input into future risk assessments, thus ensuring the cyclical nature of the risk-management process.

One reason why some organizations may disregard this important step is that they believe it to be too costly and time-consuming. The scope of any evaluation will certainly depend on the complexity of the preventive measures implemented. However, as will become evident in this chapter, an evaluation can be as simple as following up regularly with employees and tracking a few quantitative indicators of success.

Two basic questions need to be answered through this final step in the risk-management process:

1. *How effective are your reactive measures at minimizing the negative outcomes associated with incidents of violence?*
2. *How effective are your preventive measures at reducing the frequency and severity of violent incidents?*

Evaluating reactive measures

Reactive measures are implemented to help organizations respond quickly and effectively in the case of an incident of violence. In order to ensure that these measures do indeed enable an organization to respond successfully to such an incident, it is generally recommended that a post-incident evaluation, or follow-up, be conducted if and when an incident occurs.[1] A post-incident follow-up, which is distinct from an incident investigation, can provide an understanding of how and why the incident occurred and what additional measures, or modifications to existing measures, may be required. The CCOHS guide provides suggestions on how to critically examine and compare incidents of violence for the purposes of strengthening a prevention programme (box 6.1).

This excerpt suggests that the information collected in a post-incident follow-up should focus not only on identifying new or previously undefined risks, but also on determining whether the response to the incident in question was appropriate. In other words, a post-incident follow-up provides the opportunity to evaluate how well the organization responded to the incident and whether the incident response plan was followed.[2] This information can then be used to modify existing reactive measures or implement alternative measures so that the organization is better able to respond to incidents that may occur in the future. Employees who are directly and indirectly involved in the incident are likely to be the best sources of evaluation information as they can indicate whether, for example:

- the incident response was timely and well coordinated;
- the necessary treatment and/or support was provided;
- clear information was supplied;
- employees were treated fairly throughout the process;
- aspects of the response should be improved in case of future incidents.

Another important source of evaluative information is the individual, or group of individuals, responsible for responding to the incident. These individuals can indicate whether they had the resources and training necessary

---

[1] S. Perrone: *Violence in the workplace*, Research and Public Policy Series, No. 22 (Canberra, Australian Institute of Criminology, 1999), p. 88; CCOHS guide, op. cit., pp. 24–25; Berkeley guide, op. cit., pp. 95–96.

[2] D. Cherry and P. Upston: *Managing violent and potentially violent situations: A guide for workers and organizations* (Melbourne, Centre of Social Health, 1997), p. 31.

Box 6.1 Conducting incident follow-up

Incident follow-up occurs some time after the incident has been investigated and recommendations made. It involves taking a second look at the situation.

All incidents of violence should be classified according to key characteristics, such as:

- location;
- time;
- working activity or interaction (e.g. working alone and/or working off site);
- type of incident;
- outcome;
- who was involved (e.g. co-worker, client, stranger);
- possible causes.

Once the incident has been classified, you should look for similarities or common patterns. For example, do the majority of incidents occur:

- at a particular time of day (e.g. 1 to 4 a.m.)?
- during a particular time of year (e.g. report card time, Christmas)?
- inside or outside the workplace?

These observations will help you identify new or previously undefined risks and will give you opportunities to strengthen your prevention programme. Follow-up should involve establishing steps to prevent or minimize repeat occurrences.

Revisit your training and education programmes and determine if they should be redesigned or if refresher training should be provided. Outline what corrective actions are necessary and how you will achieve them.

Other points to consider:

- Did your organization implement the recommendations that were developed during the investigation phase?
- Have you gained additional insight into the situation over time?
- Are the victims OK? Do they require additional services or advice?
- Was everything done that should have been done?

Incident follow-up allows closure and assures that all the lessons that can be learned from a situation are applied to preventing future incidents.

Source: adapted from CCOHS guide, 1999, op. cit., pp. 26–27.

---

to effectively manage the incident. They can also comment on the quality of the critical incident response plan and suggest ways to improve it.

There are a number of methods for collecting information on the effectiveness of an incident response. For example, the individuals involved in the incident can be interviewed or surveyed. The Berkeley guide provides a sample of a follow-up report that can be completed some time after the incident by the victim(s) of a critical incident, or by a union representative or a manager (figure 6.1).[3] The report is intended more for incidents of physical violence than for incidents of verbal or emotional harassment. It is an evaluative tool, and is not intended to assess the well-being of the individuals involved in the incident. Organizations must ensure the physical and emotional well-being of any victims immediately following the incident and into the future.

Evaluating preventive measures

Given that the purpose of any preventive programme is to eliminate hazards and reduce the risk of violence, the evaluation of preventive measures is perhaps even more critical than the evaluation of reactive measures. Organizations must ensure that their preventive actions have been successful in reducing the occurrence and severity of violent incidents. This evaluation or review process is similar to a risk assessment in that it examines whether existing risks have been properly addressed, and whether others have been overlooked or perhaps even introduced in the prevention process.[4] If deficiencies in the prevention programme are identified through the evaluation, corrective action can then be taken, hence reinitiating the risk-management process.

The strategies outlined in the guidelines reviewed in the preparation of this book are those identified as having distilled "best practice" from authoritative and reliable sources of information. This does not, however, reduce the need for rigorous and continuing evaluation. The need for such evaluation is even more obvious when the guidance contained in these documents is applied to the specific policies and procedures put in place in a particular workplace. It cannot be emphasized too strongly or frequently that no two workplaces are the same, and that a prevention strategy which fits one workplace may not necessarily suit or operate effectively in another.

Examples

There are several documented cases of organizations that have evaluated the effectiveness of their workplace violence prevention programmes.[5] Several examples are highlighted below. Not only do they demonstrate how certain preventive measures have been shown to successfully reduce the occurrence of Type 1 and Type 2 violence, but they also provide insight into the types of statistics that can be used to track the effectiveness of a prevention programme.

* In the 1980s, the State of Victoria (Australia) implemented a number of measures to combat robberies of state betting shops, or TABs. These measures included the introduction of time-locking cash boxes, the setting

---

[3] Berkeley guide, op. cit., pp. 95–96.

[4] D. Chappell and V. Di Martino: Violence at work (Geneva, ILO, 2nd edition, 2000), pp. 124-125.

[5] Perrone, op. cit., pp. 83–84; B. Poyner and C. Warne: *Preventing violence to staff* (London, HSE, 1988), pp. 27–73.

Figure 6.1   Follow-up report: Sample form

VIOLENCE INCIDENT REPORT FORM

File a copy of this form to document the outcome of each incident or threat. The form should be completed by the employee, a union representative and/or management. For most questions in sections 1 and 2 below, circle the appropriate answer: yes, no or don't know.

Victim's name *(may use code name)*: . . . .

Company or organization: . . . .

Work location: . . . . Job title: . . . .

Phone: . . . . Age: . . . .

❏ Male   ❏ Female   Union (if any): . . . .

1. POST-INCIDENT RESPONSE

Date of incident: . . . . Time: . . . .

Immediate response and reporting

Was immediate assistance offered at the time of the incident?   Yes   No   Don't know

Type of assistance: . . . . Response time: . . . .

Was the incident reported to a supervisor or manager?   Yes   No   Don't know

Was the incident reported to the union?   Yes   No   Don't know

Was a police report filed?   Yes   No   Don't know

Was there a restraining order in effect against the person
who assaulted the employee?   Yes   No   Don't know

Was the assailant charged?   Yes   No   Don't know

Medical management

Was the employee injured?   Yes   No   Don't know

(If yes, describe injuries:) . . . .

Was the employee hospitalized?   Yes   No   Don't know

Did the employee lose any work-days?   Yes   No   Number of days: . . . .

Did the employee apply for workers' compensation?   Yes   No   Don't know

---

Counselling

Was immediate counselling provided to affected employees and witnesses who desired it?	Yes	No	Don't know
Was critical incident debriefing provided to all affected staff who desired it?	Yes	No	Don't know
Was post-trauma (follow-up) counselling provided to all affected staff who desired it?	Yes	No	Don't know
Was the victim advised about legal rights?	Yes	No	Don't know
Was all counselling provided by a professional counsellor?	Yes	No	Don't know

(Who provided counselling: ❑ *Employee Assistance Programme?*   ❑ *Union?*

    ❑ *Private agency?*   ❑ *Other?* . . . . *)*

Was counselling effective? (Give employee's opinion:)	Yes	No	Don't know

. . . .

2. ANALYSIS

Were there any warnings that this incident was going to happen?	Yes	No	Don't know

(If yes, please explain:) . . . .

Did the employee request assistance before the incident occurred?	Yes	No	Don't know

(If yes, please explain:) . . . .

Have similar incidents occurred before in this workplace?	Yes	No	Don't know

(Please describe:) . . . .

3. ACTIONS TAKEN

Describe any actions taken at the workplace (or any changes made in the violence preven-

tion programme) as a result of the incident. . . . .

Changes in incident response procedures: . . . .

Changes in security measures: . . . .

Changes in policies, procedures and training: . . . .

Other: . . . .

. . . .

Report completed by: . . . . Date: . . . .

Department/job title: . . . . Phone number: . . . .

of cash limits on selling drawers, and the fitting of adjustable time locks to main safes. The monitoring of this programme over the following decade showed a significant decline in robberies of TABs, with a corresponding increase in the robberies of banks and other commercial premises in the area.[6]

- Gainesville (Florida) enacted an ordinance mandating that convenience stores have two clerks on staff at certain times of the day. This ordinance was associated with a subsequent 92 per cent reduction in robberies between the hours of 8:00 p.m. and 4:00 a.m.[7]

- In the mid-1980s Cleveland Transit, a large municipal bus company in the United Kingdom, introduced a number of measures to prevent assaults against staff. These measures included altering the fare structure, installing protective screens, introducing mobile inspectors and providing interactive training. In the months following the installation of the protective screens and the new fare structure, there was a marked reduction in assaults, and a virtual elimination of assaults against drivers in their cabs (those incidents that the measures were specifically intended to tackle).[8]

Quantitative indicators, such as the number of robberies or assaults, were used to track the effectiveness of the preventive programme in all the examples discussed above.[9] Further, in two of these examples preventive measures were introduced to address a particular type of incident, and hence specific statistics were tracked that would assess whether the number of reported incidents of this type was reduced over time (e.g. Cleveland Transit specifically tracked the number of assaults against bus drivers, since this group had been previously identified as "high risk"). In order to monitor key indicators or statistics in this way, it is necessary for organizations to identify the key numbers that will accurately demonstrate the success or failure of their prevention programme, and implement a reliable method for tracking these numbers. This requires good internal record keeping, as is explained by OSHA in box 6.2.

These types of records can provide organizations with data (other than just incident rates) to help them accurately assess the effectiveness of their prevention programme as a whole, as well as the effectiveness of individual measures.[10] Since organizations are generally looking for either an increase or a decrease in key numbers (e.g. lowering the frequency or severity of incidents),

---

[6] Perrone, op. cit., p. 84.

[7] Florida Office of Attorney General, 1991, cited in Perrone, op. cit., p. 84.

[8] Poyner and Warne, op. cit., pp. 44–50.

[9] Incomes Data Services (IDS): *Violence against staff*, IDS Study 557 (London, 1994), p. 8, suggests other indicators, such as proportion of staff assaulted; number of days lost due to injuries sustained in a violent incident; number of employees worried about violence as measured by an employee attitude survey; number of employees mentioning violence as a factor in their decisions to leave in exit interviews. Administering a questionnaire such as Neuman and Keashly's Workplace Aggression Questionnaire (2002), or some similar instrument, can also help to establish baseline data and track progress.

[10] OSHA health care guidelines, op. cit., pp. 8–9; OSHA late-night retail guide, op. cit., p. 9.

Box 6.2   Evaluation: Record keeping

Employers can tailor their record-keeping practices to the needs of their violence prevention programme. The purpose of maintaining records is to enable the employer to monitor its ongoing efforts, to determine whether the violence prevention programme is working and to identify ways to improve it. Employers may find the following types of records useful for this purpose:

- records of employee and other injuries and illnesses at the establishment;
- records describing incidents involving violent acts and threats of such acts, even if the incident did not involve an injury or a criminal act. Records of events involving abuse, verbal attacks or aggressive behaviour can help identify patterns and risks that are not evident from the smaller set of cases that actually result in injury or crime;
- written hazard analyses;
- recommendations of police advisers, employees or consultants;
- up-to-date records of actions taken to deter violence, including work practice controls and other corrective steps;
- notes of safety meetings and training records.

Source: adapted from OSHA late-night retail guide, 1998, op. cit., p. 9.

---

several guidelines discuss the importance of establishing an initial or "baseline" rate prior to the implementation of any preventive measures. For this reason, organizations need to identify the numbers that they want to monitor, and the reports necessary to provide these data, at the same time as designing their prevention programme.

Even though preventive measures may be considered successful, as in the case of the examples discussed in this section, the evaluation process may also uncover a number of unintended consequences associated with the preventive measures. For example, it has been found that poorly designed protective screens in taxicabs may cause injury to both drivers and passengers in the event of a collision.[11] In cases such as these, the benefits linked to the preventive measures must be carefully weighed against the negative consequences also associated with these measures.

Alternative evaluation methods

Tracking quantitative indicators, such as those discussed up to this point, is not the only means of evaluating the effectiveness of a workplace violence prevention programme. Existing guidelines in this area provide a number of other suggestions. A selection is provided below:

---

[11] Perrone, op. cit., p. 84.

- Survey employees periodically to see how well they believe the preventive measures are working. This could take the form of joint management–employee meetings or could be done through a broad-based survey. Another way of eliciting employee feedback is to incorporate questions into post-incident report forms asking employees to evaluate existing measures and to suggest possible modifications. Organizations may want to consider surveying employees both before and after making job or work site changes in order to accurately assess the effectiveness of these changes.[12]
- Review the outcomes of formal workplace violence investigations and the time taken to resolve these issues.[13]
- Carry out periodic safety audits and/or hazard assessments to determine what preventive measures are in place, how well they are working and what needs to be changed.[14]
- Request periodic law enforcement or a review of the work site by an outside consultant in order to assess the effectiveness of existing preventive measures and to provide recommendations on improving employee safety.[15]
- Review any violence-related policies by holding meetings with employees and managers. During these meetings participants can discuss, for example, the relevance of the policies and how well they have been applied.[16]
- Check exit interviews and performance appraisals for signs of internal violence (Type 3), such as bullying and harassment.[17] Research suggests that a delayed exit interview (e.g. six months after departure) may be more likely to reveal bullying or other interpersonal matters.[18]

A mix of evaluation methods and data is likely to result in the strongest and most reliable programme assessment. It is generally recommended that, as a minimum, organizations identify and track one or two important quantitative indicators of success, as well as use a system whereby employees can provide regular feedback.[19] While the quantitative indicators may denote the ultimate success or failure of the programme, the feedback received from employees will provide the context necessary to fully understand these numbers, and add insight into which aspects of the programme are working and which are not. It is this feedback that will probably be most helpful in deciding which measures to keep, which to modify, and which to eliminate or replace.

---

[12] Chappell and Di Martino, op. cit., p. 124; Berkeley guide, op. cit., p. 27; Poyner and Warne, op. cit., p. 15; OSHA health care guidelines, op. cit., pp. 8–9.

[13] Ishmael with Alemoru, op. cit., p. 227.

[14] ibid.; Berkeley guide, op. cit., p. 27; OSHA health care guidelines, op. cit., pp. 8–9.

[15] OSHA health care guidelines, op. cit., p. 9.

[16] Ishmael with Alemoru, op. cit., p. 227.

[17] ibid.

[18] Neuman and Baron, 1997, op. cit.

[19] Chappell and Di Martino, op. cit., pp. 124–125; OSHA late-night retail guide, op. cit., p. 9.

Timing

Just how frequently an organization should conduct an appraisal of its workplace violence prevention programme will depend to a degree upon the circumstances prevailing in a particular organization or enterprise. For example, in certain high-risk occupations and situations the preventive measures will be considered more important than in lower-risk situations, and hence will require more frequent and intense monitoring. However, in most organizations and enterprises an annual review of a workplace violence prevention programme should be sufficient.[20]

The Western Australian code of practice provides an interesting suggestion on how to initiate and later maintain the evaluation process:

> At first, it is a good idea to deal with situations where workplace violence may occur as a specific exercise. When a system for monitoring and review is set up, it may be easier to make the management of workplace violence part of the whole safety management system where all hazards are monitored and reviewed on a regular basis.[21]

Using evaluative data

Once the evaluative data have been collected, they must be used by the organization to critically examine and improve the prevention programme. If the results suggest that the existing preventive measures are working well, the organization should probably keep them as they are. However, organizations must recognize when a measure has failed or, worse, has resulted in unintended, negative side effects. If this is the case, it is imperative that these measures be replaced or modified. Further, if the results of the appraisal suggest that violence is still a problem, the organization should consider going back to the second step in the risk-management process to identify and implement other preventive measures that may work better.[22]

Throughout this evaluation process, organizations must not forget to keep employees informed of the results and any ensuing changes to the programme. One way of accomplishing this is by sharing evaluation reports with employees. Another idea is to discuss any changes to the programme at regular employee meetings (e.g. union meetings, safety committee meetings, etc.).[23]

---

[20] CCOHS guide, op. cit., p. 30.

[21] Western Australian code of practice, op. cit., p. 20.

[22] Chappell and Di Martino, op. cit., p. 124.

[23] OSHA health care guidelines, op. cit., p. 9.

THE RISK-MANAGEMENT PROCESS IN REVIEW

7

The risk-management process

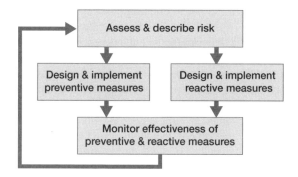

Chapters 3–6 of this book have reviewed and discussed the steps involved in the risk-management process. It is commonly agreed among practitioners in this area that by following a process such as the one presented here, an organization can develop a targeted workplace violence prevention programme that will effectively identify and address the risk factors specific to its working environment.[1] This chapter sets out to pull these steps together and to discuss the risk-management process as a whole.

First, two case studies are presented, describing organizations that have developed a workplace violence prevention programme, and in so doing have seen the risk-management process through from start to finish. Presenting these case studies should further illustrate the logical, feasible and flexible nature of the risk-management process. Second, a number of important considerations or

---

[1] B. Poyner and C. Warne: *Preventing violence to staff* (London, HSE, 1988); AFSCME, op. cit.; WorkSafe Western Australia Commission, op. cit. See Ch. 3 for a discussion of the utility of using a risk-management framework.

principles that should be kept in mind when developing a workplace violence prevention programme are discussed. The principles presented in this section were raised in a number of the influential guidelines used throughout this book, and may be used for learning purposes. Finally, the chapter discusses the importance of eliciting help and guidance from groups in the community, such as workers' organizations and law enforcement agencies, when developing, implementing and evaluating a workplace violence prevention programme. These groups can strengthen the resulting prevention programme, as well as provide resources to support an organization in its efforts.

Examples of the entire process

There are a number of documented cases of organizations that have developed workplace violence prevention programmes using the risk-management process, or a process that closely resembles it, as a guiding framework. The two case studies presented in this section (boxes 7.1 and 7.2) are taken from a recent study on violence at work by Incomes Data Services (IDS) in the United Kingdom.[2] They were chosen above the other interesting cases presented in the IDS study for two reasons: (a) both cases address the four aspects of the risk-management process presented in this book (risk assessment, preventive and reactive measures, and evaluation), even if they do so using slightly different terminology; and (b) the organizations differ on a number of important dimensions, such as industry and size. The two case studies, therefore, demonstrate how different organizations can approach the issue of workplace violence. They are intended to illustrate how two organizations have designed and implemented workplace violence prevention programmes, from risk assessment to evaluation. Given this intention, they represent "real" experiences rather than ideal scenarios.

The two case studies presented here illustrate how two separate organizations approached the task of developing and implementing a workplace violence prevention programme. Although the organizations themselves, and the nature of risk experienced in each, were different, there are a number of common themes which run through both case studies and which are important to note:

- A broad definition of workplace violence was adopted in both case studies, including incidents of physical and psychological violence.
- The first step was to identify the specific hazards in the working environments and the work groups at particular risk of experiencing incidents of violence. Both organizations then proceeded to target their prevention initiatives to the situations and groups at risk. For example, targeted training was conducted with "at risk" groups in both companies.
- Prevention was the priority in both organizations, although both also recognized the importance of implementing reactive measures (e.g. trauma counselling) in order to be prepared in the case of an incident.

---

[2] Incomes Data Services (IDS): *Violence at work*, IDS Study 628 (London, 1997), pp. 16–31.

Box 7.1   Case study: A bus company

Company A is part of a group that by acquisition has become the one of the largest bus operators in Country X. The privatized company runs a fleet of around 600 buses and coaches and employs approximately 1,700 people. The company has adopted policies in which preventive measures feature strongly.

Summer peak
Although Company A does not use a precise definition of violence, it employs a working interpretation of any unwanted act on a member of staff, whether verbal or physical. Attacks have been found to occur most frequently in the late afternoon when schools close. The number of incidents also generally climbs in the summer, when the weather is hot.

The most vulnerable staff are conductors, who number around 200. This is largely because they move freely among the passengers and, unlike drivers, cannot have any physical protection. Recent rises in the level of violence seem to have been contained, with the total for this year being 157 incidents, almost exactly the same as the previous year.

One-day induction
No formal policy document on violence is issued to staff, but at the one-day induction session they are trained in defusing difficult situations and instructed not to get involved in disputes between passengers. A video is shown to staff to back up this message. Drivers are encouraged to stay in their cabs at all costs, since the danger of getting injured increases when they leave them. If a fight breaks out on the bus, they call the police, using the direct radio link fitted to all vehicles.

Assessing the risk
Detailed risk assessments are carried out by Company A. A generic assessment applying to the whole company is supported with local assessments by the company's health and safety officer. These assessments are reviewed every one or two years and they have clearly established the major hazards which can spark off violence to bus crews. These are: (1) disputes about fares – one of the main causes of violence; (2) delays in service; (3) robberies; (4) staff attitudes; and (5) assaults by other road users, often following accidents.

Prevention is stressed
The hazards revealed by risk assessments lead automatically to the introduction of preventive measures. A number have been adopted to reduce the risk to staff, particularly protective screens on all one-person-operated buses. Together with the company's instruction to drivers not to leave their enclosed cabs, screens have contributed to a substantial reduction of assaults on drivers over the years. In addition, the design of the more modern vehicles allows screens which enclose more of the cab and offer even greater protection. Assaults on drivers are less frequent on these buses.

Other preventive steps include fitting radios. These link drivers to a central communication centre. Buses also have assault alarms which set off very audible

continued

and visible alarms on the exterior of buses. Closed-circuit television (CCTV) has been installed in some buses on routes with the highest problems, as in a recent drive to crack down on graffiti.

As local risk assessments show robbery to be one of the main motives for attacks on drivers and conductors, these staff have been provided with the facility to pay in takings during the day to reduce the amount of cash carried. Experiments have also been undertaken with personal attack alarms for conductors, although the results have so far been mixed. Robberies in bus garages have been reduced in recent years. Company A believes that the most important factor has been a big reduction in the amount of cash held on the premises. Other steps have included: the introduction of digital locking for controlling access; timed locks on safes; intruder alarms, including on fire exits; and CCTV systems.

Liaison with police is a local responsibility and some garage managers have pursued local initiatives. These have included plain clothes police travelling on bus routes troubled by fare evasion and assaults.

Safety is paramount
Company A insists that safety is the paramount consideration in the operation of its buses. Even the needs of customer care are not allowed to compromise its concentration on safety measures for both staff and passengers. Although the company's health and safety manager bears operational responsibility for safety, all employees are held responsible for putting safety measures into effect, particularly when drivers are expected to stay in the cabs for their own safety.

Targeted training
Apart from the initial training provided at the induction stage, Company A targets other training dealing with violence against employees who have a particular need. These individuals have experienced more violent incidents than the average, have had a "near miss" incident or are people that managers believe could benefit from this training. It takes the form of coaching by a trained manager either on a one-to-one basis or in small groups. The aim is to encourage the defusion of aggression or difficult situations by calming techniques, but the company steers clear of teaching self-defence.

Trauma counselling
Welfare counselling is available for all staff after a violent incident, on referral by a manager. A confidential service is provided by an outside agency, which provides a welfare adviser who can help in talking through the experience. If necessary, a victim can be sent to group counselling sessions run by a trained trauma counsellor. Victims who show signs of continuing problems such as post-traumatic stress disorder can be referred for specialist help. Cases are kept under constant review by managers, who are expected to keep in touch with staff. In some cases where victims have been afraid to get back on a bus, they have initially been accompanied by another employee to rebuild their confidence.

continued

Assault pay
Employees who need time off after a violent incident normally receive "assault pay", which is equivalent to their rostered earnings and is higher than sick pay. This is paid at the garage manager's discretion and while there is no set limit to the length of time that it can be paid, it is not intended to continue indefinitely.

Prosecution favoured
Company A has a firm policy of seeking prosecutions in cases of assault, including through the police and through private prosecution.

Regular reviews
Company A encourages employees to report all incidents. A brief description of all assaults is circulated every month among company directors, who use the data to keep violence under constant review and to see whether any new measures are needed.

Trade unions are consulted on violence through health and safety committees at each garage. Monthly meetings are held at company level between management and union representatives, chaired by the commercial director. These meetings also examine reported assaults and review procedures.

Source: adapted from Incomes Data Services (IDS): *Violence at work*, IDS Study 628 (London, 1997), pp. 27–29.

Box 7.2   Case study: a local council

Local council B in Country Y employs approximately 540 white- and blue-collar staff. Although largely rural, the council has nevertheless noticed a rise in the level of violence in recent years. Much of this increase is attributed to improved reporting, which has been accompanied by a growing awareness of violence among staff.

Council B has a clear policy on the prevention of violence to employees, which is contained in the staff handbook and is available online. The policy was added to the handbook about four years ago, mainly as a result of a fundamental review of all health and safety issues, including risk management.

A policy to prevent violence
Council B's anti-violence policy has four elements. These are: to reduce the risk to staff; to fulfil its legal obligations for the safety of staff; to provide an after-care service; and to ensure that everyone is aware of, and fulfils, their safety responsibilities to prevent violence at work.

The council's definition of violence to staff: "Any behaviour towards an employee in the course of his/her work that has detrimental, physical or psychological effects on that person". Violence is seen as covering a range of physical and non-physical acts such as threatening gestures and abusive telephone calls.

continued

Although Council B does not suffer from a large number of incidents, it has identified some high-risk areas. These include: frontline receptionists; any form of enforcement procedure, particularly areas such as interviewing for benefit fraud; revenue services such as council tax offices; planning, especially the development control arm; and outside staff such as grounds maintenance, street sweepers and environmental health officers.

Prevention is emphasized
Council B's policy places a strong emphasis on the need to prevent violence as far as possible. It attempts to strike a balance between the council's "customer care" policies and the protection of staff; therefore protective screens, which inhibit customer contact, are restricted solely to cashiers. Measures have been taken to reduce cash handling by encouraging direct debits, and cash is now handled under contract by a security firm. Security guards are also employed to provide out-of-hours protection because the civic offices remain open for committee and other meetings.

Securing office space
The emphasis on protection is also seen in the adoption of a number of measures, including regular reviews of office layouts, particularly for those areas to which the public have access. An access control system, operated by photo identity cards, has been introduced to prevent people getting into offices without permission. Installed over five years ago, the system is currently being reviewed to see whether any other provisions should be added, such as video surveillance cameras. Some cameras are already in operation in the town centre and the council is now considering whether to install them in staff car parks.

Special hazards
Departments where staff face special hazards have additional rules to protect employees. Under the basic council guidelines, employees making outside visits in an enforcement capacity, such as environmental health officers having to deal with complaints about "rave" parties, should not go out on their own. Security guards are available 24 hours a day to accompany all staff on such visits. If a security guard is not available, staff are required to ask the local police to provide an escort.

All employees who make outside visits are given mobile phones, and panic alarms are available on request. There is also a 24-hour monitoring system, run for the council by a housing association. Staff have to inform this service of their visits and expected time of return, which is later checked.

Training for those at risk
There are two stages in training staff to cope with violence. Initial training is given during induction for all employees on their first day, when they are taken through a checklist covering all corporate issues, including health and safety. Staff sign for the receipt of the council's health and safety policy, which covers violence at work.

Employees working in departments with particular risks, such as environmental health officers, are provided with more specific training. Council B runs a range of courses to meet departmental needs, including how to handle aggression, ways of defusing difficult situations, break-away techniques and coping with armed

continued

hold-ups. These courses have been run for around 150 employees. In addition, a course for home visiting has been provided, and self-defence evening courses have been offered to female staff.

Counselling network
A network of professional counsellors is available for staff who have suffered any violence, including verbal abuse, and this has been well received among the staff. Although counselling was previously provided in house by trained personnel staff, Council B now uses external counsellors because this is seen as offering greater confidentiality. A member of the council's personnel staff acts as the central coordinator and assesses the type of counselling required. Great care is taken to preserve confidentiality; even the bills sent to the council preserve anonymity.

Showing support
Council B's policy is to demonstrate support for any employee who has suffered a violent incident. A formalized procedure exists for reporting any incidents to the police, with the victim's permission, to ensure that appropriate criminal action is taken. Employees are encouraged to make a formal complaint to the police or to pursue a civil action. Financial and legal support is given by the council.

Where the police fail to take action, Council B will demonstrate its support for the employee by writing to the aggressor and warning of possible private prosecution. This may follow if recommended by the council's solicitor. However, the withdrawal of services to a violent client is constrained by the council's responsibility to provide services. Such action can only be taken after careful appraisal and discussion with the line manager.

Reporting all incidents
All types of incidents have to be reported on a standard form sent to the corporate safety adviser, who will assess the incident and, in more serious cases, pass it to the relevant departmental manager for a review of the risk assessment. The safety adviser will also notify the police and the personnel department of serious incidents. Reports of both violence and accidents are reviewed every quarter by a safety committee and the risk-management group which is linked to it. Incident recording is computerized, and the quarterly and annual reports provide a detailed breakdown that can be used to spot any trends and to identify where trouble could occur.

As part of Council B's attempts to anticipate possible problems, a "key events" list is circulated among departmental heads, so that all are aware of forthcoming important dates. For example, sending out council tax bills or summonses is likely to be followed by a rise in the number of phone calls and visits to council offices, including an increased risk of verbal abuse.

Because of its small size, Council B does not have a high level of violence against staff and has succeeded in holding the number of incidents down. In the previous year, there was only one injury through personal attack, seven cases of verbal abuse and one incident of damage to property; in the current year there were just five reports of verbal abuse and one of damage to property.

Source: adapted from IDS: *Violence at work*, op. cit., pp. 18–20.

- A mix of preventive measures was used to tackle the issue of workplace violence in both companies, as opposed to relying on one cure-all solution.
- Both organizations emphasized the importance of a strong incident reporting system, and of reviewing past incidents in an attempt to learn from these events and ultimately improve the prevention programmes.
- Both case studies discuss the delicate balance between ensuring worker safety and maintaining a high level of customer care. That is, they recognize that certain preventive measures can have an adverse impact on the provision of customer care/service, and that each measure under consideration must be critically examined from both perspectives prior to implementation.

The organizations described in the case studies covered all four components of the risk-management process. Yet they did so in slightly different ways, and emphasizing slightly different aspects. As a result, these cases illustrate the flexibility inherent in the process, and its ability to adapt to the needs of the organization in question. This is why we believe that the risk-management approach to preventing workplace violence will work for organizations in all regions and areas of the world. Regardless of the specific societal and ethnic situation in question, the four steps in the risk-management approach should facilitate the development of an effective workplace violence prevention programme. The preventive and reactive measures that are implemented may look very different in the different regions, but the process should work equally well.

Important considerations

There are a number of important points, or principles, which practitioners agree should be considered when developing a workplace violence prevention programme. Many of them have already been raised throughout this book, and a number were discussed in the context of the case studies in boxes 7.1 and 7.2. Given their importance, these points are worth revisiting:

- **A prevention strategy is only as good as the risk assessment that underlies it.** If the risk assessment is done poorly, or not at all, the resulting prevention programme will probably not address the specific hazards present in the working environment, and hence will not effectively reduce the risk of workplace violence.
- **Employee involvement is critical in the development of an effective prevention programme.** In the end, the success of any prevention programme lies in employees' willingness and ability to implement the preventive measures. The more an organization involves staff in the design and development of the prevention programme, the more willing they will be to implement and support the chosen measures. Furthermore, in those working environments where unions are present it is critical to actively involve representatives of the union throughout the prevention process.

- **The best solution will almost always be found in a mixture of different preventive measures.**
- **Organizations need to be prepared to handle an incident of violence if it occurs.** This means implementing reactive measures.
- **The evaluation of a prevention programme should examine both the effectiveness of the programme in reducing risk, and any unintended, and potentially negative, consequences associated with the measures taken.**

Support from external groups or agencies

Many businesses and government agencies lack the internal resources to prevent, detect, or manage workplace violence. For example, many small companies may not have Employee Assistance Programs (EAPs), sophisticated proprietary security personnel, or trainers to train supervisors. This lack of resources doesn't mean that these organizations should surrender and do nothing to prevent violence. In fact, there are many sources of help available to the creative and thoughtful manager: from charitable agencies ... ; from government agencies; and, in some cases, from professional organizations and trade associations.[3]

Within local communities, a wide variety of groups and agencies can help organizations to develop, implement and evaluate their workplace violence prevention programmes.[4] When conducting a risk assessment, for example, valuable data on the experience of violence in businesses in the same industry and/or area can be obtained from relevant industry organizations and union offices. Further, local businesses can work together to reduce the risk of violence in their community (e.g. shopkeepers can look out for neighbouring shops).[5] Moreover, numerous community mental health resources can provide consultation during critical incident preparation, and conduct debriefing sessions following a violent incident (many of these resources are available at a very low cost).

Possibly the most valuable resource when developing a workplace violence prevention programme is the local police department. There is much that the police can do to assist in developing effective workplace violence prevention strategies at the local level. There is growing recognition among law enforcement officials that the enhanced police response to domestic violence over recent years should now be emulated in the area of workplace violence. For example, a statement by the International Association of Chiefs of Police (IACP) recommends that law enforcement agencies develop effective workplace violence prevention programmes in their own departments, as well

---

[3] J. Kinney: *Violence at work: How to make your company safe for employees and customers* (Englewood Cliffs, NJ, Prentice Hall, 1995), p. 143.

[4] CCOHS guide, op. cit., p. 29.

[5] IDS: *Disciplinary procedures*, IDS Study 640 (London, 1997), p. 3.

as assisting with the development of these programmes in the community.[6] In order to take advantage of this assistance, organizations need to understand how police agencies might be able to assist them in their efforts to combat workplace violence. This assistance can include, but is not limited to, the provision of:[7]

- information concerning police department resources, including a central point of contact in the department who will answer questions and address concerns;
- guidelines and examples of how and when to contact the police department in matters involving workplace violence;
- advice on preventive measures that can be tailored to the needs of small businesses;
- assistance in improving physical security and the prevention of acts of violence;
- assistance in ensuring that an organization's critical incident response plan is capable of dealing with emergency situations; and
- a coordinated critique of an organization's response after each serious incident of workplace violence.

The IACP provides several other useful suggestions (box 7.3).

Box 7.3   Take advantage of community resources

There are many programmes and resources in the community that can help you develop your workplace violence plans. Some examples follow:

- Invite local police into your firm to promote good relations and to help them become more familiar with your facility. The police can explain what actions they typically take during incidents involving threats and violence. Such visits can help your firm work better with the police when incidents do occur.
- Use law enforcement and security experts to educate employees on how to prevent violence in the workplace. Such experts can provide crime prevention information, conduct building security inspections, and teach employees how to avoid being a victim.
- Consider using local associations and community organizations, such as the Chamber of Commerce, security organizations and law enforcement groups, as a resource in order to stay abreast of crime trends and prevention techniques. Communicate to your employees those issues and trends that pose a significant threat.

Source: adapted from IACP, 1998, op. cit., sect. 2, p. 1.

---

[6] International Association of Chiefs of Police (IACP): *Combating workplace violence: Guidelines for employers and law enforcement* (Washington, DC, 1998), p. 1
(htttp://www.theiacp.org/documents/pdfs/Publications/combatingworkplaceviolence.pdf).

[7] ibid.

Clearly there is a large and valuable pool of local resources that can help organizations in their efforts to prevent workplace violence, be it providing useful information during the risk-assessment phase, or suggestions on the most appropriate security measures during the implementation of preventive measures. Not only can these local groups and agencies provide expert information to strengthen a prevention programme, but they can also become an active part of the internal team responsible for the success of the programme. This type of help can prove particularly useful for small businesses, which might otherwise find it difficult to allocate internal resources to conduct the various phases of the risk-management process.

CONCLUSION

8

Over the last decade violence at work has gained momentum as a priority issue for governments, trade unions and employers. It is an issue that can affect any organization, regardless of its size, industry or geographical location. Workplace violence is truly a problem of global dimensions and, as a result, employers around the world are looking for ways to protect their employees. This book responds to this need by providing practical guidance to all those individuals, groups and organizations engaged in combating violence at work.

Research and experience demonstrates that steps can be taken to prevent the occurrence of violence within organizations. This book delineates the steps in the risk-management process and discusses each in detail. By following the steps presented, organizations can develop targeted workplace violence prevention programmes that will effectively address the risk factors specific to their working environments. These steps, and the guidance provided throughout this book, are based on an analysis of existing international resources and, in particular, policies and guidelines that have been developed across a range of workplaces to tackle this important issue. What results is a presentation of the full range of responses and approaches that can be used to respond to and prevent violence at work. It is important to remember, however, that the sources of the resources and guidelines used throughout this book were generally based in the industrialized countries of the world, primarily in Europe and North America.

It is hoped that readers will come away from this book with a better understanding of how groups and organizations approach this serious problem. Moreover, it is hoped that they will come away believing that it is indeed possible and necessary to take steps to reduce the risk of workplace violence. Some of the keys to reducing this risk include:

- **recognizing the importance of a preventive focus.** While it is important to have a critical incident response plan in order to be able to respond effectively in the case of an incident of violence, the priority should always be placed on implementing measures that will help to prevent incidents;

- **adopting a systematic approach to violence at work,** beginning with an appraisal of the nature and scope of the problem and proceeding to the design, implementation and monitoring of appropriate interventions. The risk-management process presented and discussed in this book represents such an approach. This process provides organizations with the flexibility needed to develop prevention programmes suited to their individual needs. Furthermore, a systematic approach such as the one presented here need not be expensive or complicated. Simple measures such as changes to the design of the working environment or to the patterns of work can go a long way towards protecting workers;

- **identifying and implementing a variety of preventive measures.** Organizations need to consider the range of factors that may contribute to the occurrence of violence in their working environment, and target measures that will address each of these key contributing factors;

- **involving workers and union representatives throughout the process.** Worker and union involvement is critical to the development of an effective violence prevention programme;

- **understanding that since no two organizations are identical, no two prevention programmes should be identical**. The guidelines and examples discussed throughout this book provide interesting case studies from which to work, but are not intended to serve as off-the-shelf template solutions. When developing a workplace violence prevention programme, it is imperative that organizations implement measures that will address the hazards specific to their own working environments;

- **ensuring that any workplace violence prevention programme is developed and implemented in alignment with existing legislation.** Organizations must understand the legal requirements within their country or jurisdiction and, in particular, any legislation relating to the prevention of workplace violence.

Moving forward

The challenge of preventing workplace violence falls on many different groups. National governments, for example, need to develop and enforce legal provisions that will address the issue of workplace violence. Governments can play an important role in encouraging both the public and private sectors to implement the changes necessary to produce a workplace free of violence (e.g. providing organizations with the resources to develop violence prevention programmes; requiring organizations that receive funding to have violence prevention programmes in place as a condition of their contract with the government).[1] Trade unions and employee groups also have an important part

---

[1] United States Department of Health and Human Services, Substance Abuse and Mental Health Services Administration: *Center for mental health services forum report: Preventing violence in the workplace* (Washington, DC, 1994), p. 12.

to play in the prevention of workplace violence. These groups can work to influence employers and supplement any existing or new legal provisions through the collective bargaining process. Further, these groups can provide important information and guidance on how to develop workplace violence prevention programmes (e.g. by distributing case studies of companies that are working to prevent violence).

Perhaps most importantly, employers need to take steps to prevent the occurrence of violence within their premises. While it is recognized that it is not the role of employers to tackle the underlying issues of violence in society, it is clear that much can and should be done by organizations to reduce the risk of violence within their own working environments. "A concerned administration that implements and maintains a well developed [violence prevention] programme should be able to succeed in reducing the incidence of assaults and injuries in the workplace."[2]

This book provides concrete guidance on how to design, implement and evaluate such a programme. Furthermore, it illustrates how other organizations have approached this serious occupational issue and provides helpful tools which can be used along the way. It is now time for employers and workers to work together to initiate the violence prevention process and to engage in the fight against workplace violence. It is time for governments to facilitate such initiatives by creating a supportive policy and regulatory environment. It is time to adapt the risk-management process to suit the needs of individual enterprises. It is time to eliminate or minimize the hazards that put workers at risk. It is time to provide workers with a secure working environment, one that encourages respect, equal treatment, and productive and safe working relationships.

---

[2] California Department of Industrial Relations (Cal/OSHA): *Guidelines for security and safety of health care and community service workers* (San Francisco, CA, Division of Occupational Safety and Health, State of California, 1994), Preface.

Appendix A

Statistics

The statistics presented here bear witness to the scale, severity and cost of workplace violence in the United States and Europe (the two regions of the world which document this form of violence in greatest detail). It is important to interpret these statistics with caution given the variation in reporting and data collection procedures, and in the definitions of workplace violence used. These figures, and the studies that produced them, are discussed in detail in the ILO publication, *Violence at work*.[1]

United States

• According to the National Institute for Occupational Safety and Health (NIOSH), in 1996 homicide was the second leading cause of death on the job, after motor vehicle accidents.[2]

• The 1992–96 National Crime Victimization Survey suggests that American residents experience more than 2 million violent victimizations at work each year – 1.4 million simple assaults, 395,000 aggravated assaults, 50,000 rapes and sexual assaults, and 53,000 robberies.[3]

• A study by the National Safe Workplace Institute estimated that the total costs to employers for workplace violence amounted to more than US$4 billion in 1992.[4]

• A 1993 survey by Northwest National Life Insurance sampled 600 full-time workers and concluded that one in four workers reported being harassed, threatened or physically attacked on the job in the previous 12 months.[5]

• A statewide survey of Michigan residents in 2000 reported that about 59 per cent of the representative working sample indicated they had experienced at least one type of emotionally abusive behaviour at the hands of fellow workers.[6]

[1] D. Chappell and V. Di Martino: *Violence at work* (Geneva, ILO, 2nd edition, 2000), Ch. 2.

[2] NIOSH: *NIOSH report addresses problem of workplace violence, suggests strategies for preventing risks*, press release (Washington, DC, 8 July 1996); http://www.cdc.gov/niosh/violpr.html.

[3] United States Department of Justice, Bureau of Justice Statistics: *Workplace violence, 1992–96: National crime victimization survey* (Washington, DC, 1998).

[4] J. Kinney: *Violence at work: How to make your company safe for employees and customers* (Englewood Cliffs, NJ, Prentice Hall, 1995), p. 18.

[5] NWNL: *Fear and violence in the workplace: A survey documenting the experience of American workers* (Minneapolis, MN, 1993).

[6] L. Keashly and K. Jagatic: *The nature, extent and impact of emotional abuse in the workplace: Results of a statewide study*, unpublished paper presented at an Academy of Management conference, Toronto, 2000.

Europe

- The results of a 1996 survey of workers throughout the European Union, conducted by the European Foundation for the Improvement of Living and Working Conditions, indicated that 4 per cent of workers (6 million) were subjected to physical violence, 2 per cent (3 million workers) to sexual harassment, and 8 per cent (12 million workers) to intimidation and bullying.[7]

- The 1998 British Crime Survey (BCS) estimated that there were just over 1.2 million incidents of violence at work in England and Wales in 1997.[8]

- In 2000, Hoel & Cooper conducted a national study in the United Kingdom and estimated that 2.5 million people can be considered as labelling themselves as having been bullied during the last six months.[9]

- Several surveys in Finland have shown that approximately 10 per cent of the workers interviewed have experienced some form of bullying.[10]

---

[7] Data kindly provided by Mr. Pascal Paoli, Project Manager, European Foundation for the Improvement of Living and Working Conditions, Dublin, 1997.

[8] T. Budd: *Violence at work: Findings from the British Crime Survey* (London, Home Office, 1999), p. a. For a more detailed review of the trends reported in work-related crime in England and Wales during the 1990s, see H. Standing and D. Nicolini: *Review of workplace-related violence* (London, HSE, 1997), Ch. 2.

[9] C. Rayner, H. Hoel and C. L. Cooper: *Workplace bullying: What we know, who is to blame, and what can we do?* (London, Taylor & Francis, 2002).

[10] M. Vartia: "Bullying at workplaces", in *Research on violence, threats and bullying as health risks among health care personnel*, Proceedings of the Workshop for Nordic Researchers, 14–16 August 1994 (Reykjavik, 1995).

APPENDIX B

Searching for explanations

Easy access to weapons,[1] watching violent media,[2] suffering incivility,[3] experiencing chronic anger,[4] living through downsizings and other work-related stressors[5] – the search for explanations of workplace violence continues at the popular and the professional levels of society. For many scientists this search is beginning to produce results that go beyond the single or simplistic explanations favoured by many members of the public. It is now widely recognized by the scientific community engaged in violence-related research that the causes of this behaviour are complex and defy easy description.[6] As one recent study of workplace violence has reported, an understanding of this particular form of aggression has now moved beyond a focus on the individual assailant or victim, and towards an emphasis on organizational and contextual factors. The study provides three reasons for this shift in focus:

> First, there is a need to move beyond the idea that violence in the workplace is mostly a random occurrence to be regarded as a "misfortune". Experience derived from the related field of work safety suggests in fact that attributing events to chance or "misfortune" is usually associated with a reduced effort to explore the issue in search of appropriate countermeasures. Accordingly, if it is assumed that violence is much less randomly distributed than is sometimes depicted by the media, and that risk can be related to some specific social and geographical factors, it then becomes possible to be proactive in developing preventive strategies.

> Second, shifting the focus from the offender/victim interaction to the broader societal and organizational context makes it possible to focus on the more hidden relationships between violent acts, the organization and/or community response, and frequency or recurrence of offences ...

---

[1] J.M. Broder and K.Q. Seelye: "Clinton's violence tack avoids two big lobbies", in *International Herald Tribune*, 6 Nov. 1999.

[2] L. Mifflin: "A media–violence link? Washington seeks answers after massacre", in *International Herald Tribune*, 5 Oct. 1999.

[3] See L.M. Andersson and C.M. Pearson: "Tit for tat: The spiralling effect of incivility in the workplace", in *Academy of Management Review*, Vol. 24, 1999, pp. 452–471. See also C.M. Pearson, L.M. Andersson and C. Porath: "Assessing and attacking workplace incivility", in *Organizational Dynamics*, Vol. 29, No. 2, 2000, pp. 123–137.

[4] See D.E. Gibson and S.G. Barsade: *The experience of anger at work: Lessons from the chronically angry*, paper presented at an Academy of Management conference, Chicago, 11 Aug. 1999, pp. 3, 7–8. The paper reports on the findings of a national telephone survey of 1,000 American adults, aged 18 or older, who were employed either full time or part time. The survey was conducted through the Gallup Organization.

[5] J.H. Neuman and R.A. Baron: "Aggression in the workplace", in R.A. Giacalone and J. Greenberg: *Antisocial behavior in organizations* (Thousand Oaks, CA, Sage Publications, 1997), pp. 37–67; J. Barling: "The prediction, experience, and consequences of workplace violence", in E.Q. Bulatao and G.R. VandenBos (eds.): *Violence on the job: Identifying risks and developing solutions* (Washington, DC, American Psychological Association, 1996), pp. 29–49; E.Q. Bulatao and G.R.VandenBos: "Workplace violence: Its scope and the issues", ibid., pp. 1–23.

[6] Chappell and Di Martino, op. cit., Chs. 1–3.

Third, in the last decade, a more finely grained knowledge of the contexts within which violence occurs has developed, as has an associated body of knowledge about appropriate preventive strategies at the organizational level. Frameworks thus need to reflect the linkages which can now be made between incident identification and prevention.[7]

In the ILO publication *Violence at work* an extensive review was made of the "more finely grained knowledge" now available concerning the context within which workplace violence can occur.[8] That review concluded that the most promising approach to an understanding of workplace violence is to be found in an interactive analysis of both individual and social risk factors, with particular attention being given to the situational context in which certain types of work tasks are performed.

In reaching this conclusion, the ILO publication was influenced to a significant degree by a special study of violence at work, conducted in 1988 by the London-based Tavistock Institute of Human Relations on behalf of the United Kingdom's Health and Safety Executive.[9] The study recognized that a number of factors can cause or contribute to a risk of violence at work:

> The problem may lie in the assailant, in that there may be something about him which makes him strike out at the employee. The employee may be partly to blame because of incompetence or because of an unsympathetic attitude, or the way the organization works may sometimes lead to misunderstanding or frustration.[10]

The Tavistock researchers developed a model that brought together the various factors that they found to be relevant in explaining how an interaction between an assailant (perpetrator) and an employee (victim) produced a violent outcome in the workplace. The Tavistock model, as it has come to be known, was revised and expanded upon by Chappell and Di Martino in *Violence at work*.[11] Their modified model is shown in figure A1.

This model illustrates the range of risk factors that can contribute to the occurrence of workplace violence. For example, it points out that individual factors are often associated with perpetrators of workplace violence, such as a history of violence, being male and being a young adult. Similarly, there are factors or attributes of the victim that can be associated with the risk of violence, such as level of skill and experience.

The model goes further to illustrate those factors within the workplace that can influence the risk of violence. These workplace risk factors can be related

---

[7] Standing and Nicolini, op. cit., p. 31.

[8] Chappell and Di Martino, op. cit., Ch. 3.

[9] B. Poyner and C. Warne: *Preventing violence to staff* (London, HSE, 1988), p. 2. It should be noted that almost a decade after the appearance of this initial study the Tavistock Institute released an updated report on the subject (Standing and Nicolini, op. cit.). This report refined the model which was developed in the original study.

[10] Poyner and Warne, op. cit., p. 2.

[11] Chappell and Di Martino, op. cit., p. 63.

to the working environment, or to the circumstances or situations under which employees perform their specific tasks or duties. Aspects of the working environment that can precede an incident of violence include not only elements of the physical environment (e.g. the way offices or waiting-rooms are set up), but also organizational events and strategies, such as downsizings and a shift to a contingent workforce. Research shows that these organizational strategies and aspects of the organizational culture (e.g. an authoritarian management style) can increase the probability of worker-to-worker violence.[12] So too can task-specific factors (e.g. working alone can increase vulnerability, as can working with people in distress).

Lastly, the model illustrates the negative outcomes or consequences often linked to the experience of workplace violence. For the victims, these outcomes can include physical and/or psychological ailments. For the enterprise, an incident of workplace violence can result in a loss in productivity, increased absenteeism, and damage to its image and reputation.[13]

It is clear from this model, and from the research that underlies it, that there are a number of important factors and circumstances which contribute to the occurrence of workplace violence. All these factors must be kept in mind when trying to understand this phenomenon and, even more importantly, when trying to respond to it. Hence, the most effective workplace violence prevention programmes are likely to be those that take an integrative approach to identifying preventive measures, considering the assailant, the employee (victim) and, most importantly, the workplace as potential points of intervention.

---

[12] Neuman and Baron, 1997, op. cit.; J.A. Kinney and D.L. Johnson: *Breaking point: The workplace violence epidemic and what to do about it* (Chicago, IL, National Safe Workplace Institute, 1993).

[13] A more detailed description and explanation of the Chappell and Di Martino model, including a description of the modifications that were made to the original Tavistock model, can be found in Chappell and Di Martino, op. cit., pp. 62–78; Barling, op. cit.

Figure A1   Workplace violence: An interactive model

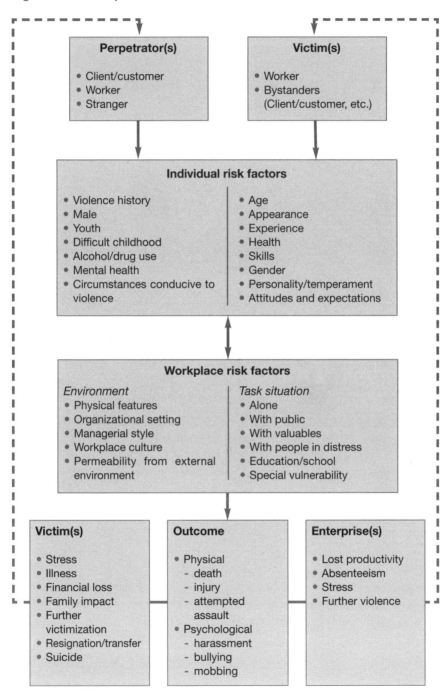

BIBLIOGRAPHY

American Federation of State, County and Municipal Employees (AFSCME), AFL-CIO: *Preventing workplace violence* (Washington, DC, 1998) (http://www.afscme.org/health/violtc.htm).

Andersson, L.M.; Pearson, C.M. "Tit for tat: The spiralling effect of incivility in the workplace", in *Academy of Management Review*, Vol. 24, 1999, pp. 452–471.

Ashforth, B. "Petty tyranny in organizations", in *Human Relations*, Vol. 47, No. 7, 1994, pp. 755–778.

Australian Public Service Commission. *Eliminating workplace harassment guidelines* (Canberra, Australian Government Publishing Service, 1994).

Barling, J. "The prediction, experience, and consequences of workplace violence", in E.Q. Bulatao and G.R. VandenBos (eds.): *Violence on the job: Identifying risks and developing solutions* (Washington, DC, American Psychological Association, 1996), pp. 29–49.

Baron, R.A.; Neuman, J.H. "Workplace violence and workplace aggression: Evidence on their relative frequency and potential causes", in *Aggressive Behavior*, Vol. 22, 1996, pp. 161–173.

Beale, D.; Cox, T.; Leather, P. "Work-related violence: Is national reporting good enough?", in *Work and Stress*, Vol. 10, No. 2, 1996, pp. 99–103.

Broder, J.M.; Seelye, K.Q. "Clinton's violence tack avoids two big lobbies", in *International Herald Tribune*, 6 Nov. 1999.

Budd, T. *Violence at work: Findings from the British Crime Survey* (London, Home Office, 1999).

Bulatao, E.Q.; VandenBos, G.R. "Workplace violence: Its scope and the issues", in E.Q. Bulatao and G.R. VandenBos (eds.): *Violence on the job: Identifying risks and developing solutions* (Washington, DC, American Psychological Association, 1996), pp. 1–23.

Buss, A.H. *The psychology of aggression* (New York, Wiley, 1961).

California Department of Industrial Relations, Division of Occupational Safety and Health Administration (Cal/OSHA). *Guidelines for security and safety of health care and community service workers* (San Francisco, CA, 1994).

—. *Guidelines for workplace security* (San Francisco, CA, 1995) (http://165.235.90.100/DOSH/dosh_publications/worksecurity.html).

Canadian Centre for Occupational Health and Safety (CCOHS). *Violence in the workplace: Prevention guide* (Hamilton, Ontario, 2nd edition, 2001) (www.ccohs.ca).

Chappell, D.; Di Martino, V. *Violence at work* (Geneva, ILO, 2nd edition, 2000). Also available in French: *La violence au travail* (Genève, BIT, 2000).

Cherry, D.; Upston, P. *Managing violent and potentially violent situations: A guide for workers and organizations* (Melbourne, Centre of Social Health, 1997).

Commerce Clearing House (CCH) International. "Managing violence and traumatic incidents at work", in *Managing Organizational Safety and Health* (North Ryde, 1995), Sect. 39, pp. 701–793.

Cowie, H., et al. "Measuring workplace bullying", in *Aggression and Violent Behavior*, Vol. 7, 2002, pp. 33–51.

Di Martino, V.; Gold, D.; Schaap, A. *Managing emerging health-related problems at work: SOLVE – stress, tobacco, alcohol and drugs, HIV/AIDS, violence* (Geneva, ILO, 2002).

Fox, S.; Spector, P.E.; Miles, D. "Counterproductive work behavior (CWB) in response to job stressors and organizational justice: Some mediator and moderator tests for autonomy and emotions", in *Journal of Vocational Behavior*, Vol. 59, 2001, pp. 291–309.

Gallagher, J. *Violent times: A health and safety report* (London, Trades Union Congress, 1999).

Gibson, D.E.; Barsade, S.G. *The experience of anger at work: Lessons from the chronically angry,* paper presented at an Academy of Management conference, Chicago, 11 Aug. 1999.

Gleninning, P.M. "Workplace bullying: Curing the cancer of the American workplace", in *Public Personnel Management*, Vol. 30, No. 3, 2001, pp. 269–286.

Health and Safety Executive (HSE). *Violence at work: A guide for employers* (London, 1997) (http://www.hse.gov.uk/pubns/indg69.pdf).

Incomes Data Services (IDS). *Disciplinary procedures*, IDS Study 640 (London, 1997).

— . *Violence against staff*, IDS Study 557 (London, 1994).

— . *Violence at work*, IDS Study 628 (London, 1997).

Industrial Relations Service (IRS). "Bullying at work: A survey of 157 employers", in *Employee Health Bulletin*, Vol. 8, Apr. 1999.

International Air Transport Association (IATA). *Guidelines for handling disruptive/unruly passengers* (Geneva, 1998).

International Association of Chiefs of Police (IACP). *Combating workplace violence: Guidelines for employers and law enforcement* (Washington, DC, 1998) (htttp://www.theiacp.org/documents/pdfs/Publications/combatingworkplaceviolence.pdf).

International Labour Office (ILO). *Annotated bibliography on violence at work* (Geneva, 1999).

— . *Guidelines on occupational safety and health management systems, ILO–OSH* (Geneva, 2001).

International Transport Workers' Federation (ITF), Civil Aviation Section. *Air rage: The prevention and management of unruly passenger behaviour,* Safety in Practice, No. 1 (London, 2000) (http://www.itf.org.uk).

Ishmael, A.; Alemoru, B. *Harassment, bullying and violence at work: A practical guide to combating employee abuse* (London, The Industrial Society, 1999).

Keashly, L. "Emotional abuse in the workplace: Conceptual and empirical issues", in *Journal of Emotional Abuse*, Vol. 1, 1998, pp. 85–117.

Keashly, L.; Jagatic, K. "By any other name: American perspectives on workplace bullying", in S. Einarsen et al. (eds.): *Bullying and emotional abuse in the workplace: International perspectives on research and practice* (London, Taylor & Francis, 2003).

—; —. *The nature, extent, and impact of emotional abuse in the workplace: Results of a statewide survey,* unpublished paper presented at an Academy of Management conference, Toronto, 2000.

Kinney, J. *Violence at work: How to make your company safe for employees and customers* (Englewood Cliffs, NJ, Prentice Hall, 1995).

Kinney, J.A.; Johnson, D.L. *Breaking point: The workplace violence epidemic and what to do about it* (Chicago, IL, National Safe Workplace Institute, 1993).

Labig, C.E. (RHR International Co.). *Preventing violence in the workplace* (New York, American Management Association, 1995).

Leymann, H. "Mobbing and psychological terror at workplaces", in *Violence and Victims*, Vol. 5, No. 2, 1990, pp. 119–126.

Mifflin, L. "A media–violence link? Washington seeks answers after massacre", in *International Herald Tribune*, 5 Oct. 1999.

National Institute for Occupational Safety and Health (NIOSH). *NIOSH report addresses problem of workplace violence, suggests strategies for preventing risks,* press release (Washington, DC, 8 July 1996) (http://www.cdc.gov/niosh/violpr.html)).

Neuman, J.E; Baron, R.A. "Workplace violence and workplace aggression: Evidence concerning specific forms, potential causes, and preferred targets", in *Journal of Management*, Vol. 24, No. 3, 1998, pp. 391–419.

—; —. "Aggression in the workplace", in R.A. Giacalone and J. Greenberg: *Antisocial behavior in organizations* (Thousand Oaks, CA, Sage Publications, 1997), pp. 37–67.

Neuman, J.H.; Keashly, L. *Development of a measure of workplace aggression and violence: The Workplace Aggression Research Questionnaire (WAR-Q),* unpublished paper, 2002.

Northwestern National Life Insurance Company (NWNL). *Fear and violence in the workplace: A survey documenting the experience of American workers* (Minneapolis, MN, 1993).

Pearson, C.M.; Andersson, L.M.; Porath, C. "Assessing and attacking workplace incivility", in *Organizational Dynamics*, Vol. 29, No. 2, 2000, pp. 123–137.

Perrone, S. *Violence in the workplace*, Research and Public Policy Series, No. 22 (Canberra, Australian Institute of Criminology, 1999).

Poyner, D., Warne, C. *Preventing violence to staff* (London, HSE, 1988).

Rayner, C.; Hoel, H.; Cooper, C.L. *Workplace bullying: What we know, who is to blame, and what can we do?* (London, Taylor & Francis, 2002).

Robinson, S.L.; Bennett, R.J. "A typology of deviant workplace behaviors: A multi-dimensional scaling study", in *Academy of Management Journal*, Vol. 38, No. 2, 1995, pp. 555–572.

Rogers, K.A. *Toward an integrative understanding of workplace mistreatment*, unpublished M.A. dissertation (Guelph, Ontario, University of Guelph, 1998).

—; Kelloway, E.K. "Violence at work: Personal and organizational outcomes", in *Journal of Occupational Health Psychology*, Vol. 12, 1997, pp. 63–71.

Standing, H.; Nicolini, D. *Review of workplace-related violence* (London, HSE, 1997).

Trades Union Congress (TUC). *Beat bullying at work: A guide for trade union representatives and personnel managers* (London, 1998).

UNISON. *Violence at work: A guide to risk prevention for UNISON branches, stewards and safety representatives* (London, 1997) (http://www.unison.org.uk).

United States Department of Health and Human Services, Substance Abuse and Mental Health Services Administration. *Center for mental health services forum report: Preventing violence in the workplace* (Washington, DC, 1994).

United States Department of Justice, Bureau of Justice Statistics. *Workplace violence, 1992–96: National crime victimization survey* (Washington, DC, 1998).

United States Department of Labor, Occupational Safety and Health Administration (OSHA). *Guidelines for preventing workplace violence for health care and social service workers* (Washington, DC, 1998).

—. *Recommendations for workplace violence prevention programs in late-night retail establishments* (Washington, DC, 1998) (http://www.osha-slc.gov/SLTC/workplaceviolence/latenight/).

—. "Safety and health program management guidelines", in *Federal Register*, Vol. 54, 26 Jan. 1989.

—. *Workplace violence awareness and prevention* (Washington, DC, 1998) (http://www.osha-slc.gov/workplace_violence/wrkplaceViolence.Table.html).

United States Department of Labor, Occupational Safety and Health Administration (OSHA); Long Island Coalition for Workplace Violence Awareness and Prevention. *Workplace violence awareness and prevention: An information and instructional package for use by employers and employees* (Washington, DC, 1996) (http://www.osha-slc.gov/workplace_violence/wrkplaceViolence.intro.html).

United States Office of Personnel Management, Office of Workplace Relations. *Dealing with workplace violence: A guide for agency planners*, doc. No. OWR-09 (Washington, DC, 1998) (http://www.opm.gov/workplac/pdf/full.pdf).

University of California at Berkeley, Labor Occupational Health Program. *Violence on the job: A guidebook for labor and management* (Berkeley, CA, Center for Occupational and Environmental Health, 1997) (http://socrates.berkeley.edu/~lohp/Publications/ Violence-on-the-job/violence-on-the-job.htm).

Vartia, M. "Bullying at workplaces", in *Research on violence, threats and bullying as health risks among health care personnel,* Proceedings of the Workshop for Nordic Researchers, 14–16 Aug.1994 (Reykjavik, 1995).

Workcover New South Wales; National Children's and Youth Law Centre (NCYLC). *Workplace violence: Intervention strategies for your business. A secure workplace for young Australians* (Sydney, 2000, 2001) (http://www.workcover.nsw. gov.au/html/bullying.asp).

Workers' Compensation Board of British Columbia (WCBBC). *Take care: How to develop and implement a workplace violence program* (Vancouver, 2001) (http://www.worksafebc.com/publications/publication-index/t.asp).

WorkSafe Western Australia Commission. *Workplace violence: Code of practice* (Perth, Government of Western Australia, 1999) (http://www.safetyline.wa.gov.au).

Wynne, R. et al. *Guidance on the prevention of violence at work* (Brussels, European Commission, Employment and Social Affairs, 1997)

INDEX

Note: Page numbers in **bold** refer to major text sections, those in *italic* to boxes and figures. Subscript numbers appended to a page number indicate a footnote reference.